ISBN 978-1-6671-2834-4

THE SOCIALIST PARTY OF GREAT BRITAIN

OBJECT   The establishment of a system of society based upon the common ownership and democratic control of the means and instruments for producing and distributing wealth by and in the interest of the whole community.

DECLARATION OF PRINCIPLES

The Socialist Party of Great Britain holds:—

1. That Society as at present constituted is based upon the ownership of the means of living (i.e., land, factories, railways, etc.) by the capitalist or master class, and the consequent enslavement of the working class, by whose labour alone wealth is produced.

2. That in society, therefore, there is an antagonism of interests, manifesting itself as a class struggle, between those who possess but do not produce, and those who produce but do not possess.

3. That this antagonism can be abolished only by the emancipation of the working class from the domination of the master class, by the conversion into the common property of society of the means of production and distribution, and their democratic control by the whole people.

4. That as in the order of social evolution the working class is the last class to achieve its freedom, the emancipation of the working class will involve the emancipation of all mankind without distinction of race or sex.

5. That this emancipation must be the work of the working class itself.

6. That as the machinery of government, including the armed forces of the nation, exists only to conserve the monopoly by the capitalist class of the wealth taken from the workers, the working class must organise consciously and politically for the conquest of the powers of government, national and local, in order that this machinery, including these forces, may be converted from an instrument of oppression into the agent of emancipation and the overthrow of privilege, aristocratic and plutocratic.

7. That as all political parties are but the expression of class interests, and as the interest of the working class is diametrically opposed to the interests of all sections of the master class, the party seeking working-class emancipation must be hostile to every other party.

8. THE SOCIALIST PARTY of Great Britain, therefore, enters the field of political action determined to wage war against all other political parties, whether alleged labour or avowedly capitalist, and calls upon the members of the working class of this country to muster under its banner to the end that a speedy termination may be wrought to the system which deprives them of the fruits of their labour, and that poverty may give place to comfort, privilege to equality, and slavery to freedom.

Those agreeing with the above principles and desire enrolment in the Party should apply for membership form to secretary of nearest branch or at Head Office.

THE BIRTH OF THE SOCIALIST PARTY

In the early days of the Working Class Movement, when advocates of better conditions were treated as felons, there was some ground for engaging in secret societies and for defending internal deliberations from prying eyes. Towards the end of the Nineteenth Century the fetters upon revolutionary activity had been so considerably loosened in England, and the path to power opened by means of electoral action, that secrecy was no longer necessary and only became an obstacle to progress.

But the tradition of secrecy still persisted in the social democratic parties, and, along with the fetish of leadership, placed in the hands of small groups of leaders power to influence the policy of parties in the directions they wished. The result of this was that policy was decided by a few people in prominent positions. This had a retarding influence upon the growth of the workers understanding and upon the real progress of the working class movement. Those in the forefront of the movement felt that they were the nature-designed leaders of a great cause, and they were impatient to build up a large following, believing that this in itself would bring about the emancipation of the workers; the familiar picture of leaders selling out for pelf and place only existed in outline. Moreover, those who were at that time determining the policy of the movement in different directions were tied to reformist programmes; some of them denied the existence of the class struggle and saw in Socialism nothing more than the establishment of eternal principles of justice and morality.

Inside the Social Democratic Federation, the most advanced of the English radical parties, dissatisfaction with the reformist programmes and the temporary agreements with capitalist parties was growing and had already been responsible for an ill-fated breakaway led by William Morris, Belfort Bax, Frederick Lessner, and Marx's daughter Eleanor, at the end of the eighties. They had formed the Socialist League which had the blessing of Frederick Engels. Unfortunately the " League " went to the other extreme and abandoned parliamentary action, eventually coming under the control of anarchists.

During the early days of the present century a group of young people began to form which aimed at clarifying the position and transforming the Social Democratic Federation into a genuine Socialist organisation, free from the fetters of reformism. They made fierce protests against reformism, leadership, private agreements and political trading at meetings and conferences. Their efforts, however, were paralysed by the power, influences and secret arrangements of the official leaders, who dubbed the militant group " Impossiblists " on the ground that their proposals were unpractical, unsound, and would make the movement impotent.

About the same time the ideas of the American Socialist Labour Party, headed by a very able speaker and writer, Daniel de Leon, were making some headway amongst youthful radicals in England and Scotland in spite of the fact that this organisation was also crippled by a reformist bias and by a leaning towards industrial unionism.

In 1903 and 1904 the "Impossiblist" group made desperate efforts by " boring from within " tactics to head off the reformist policy of the leaders, but without success. The latter became so incensed at the attacks upon them that they finally arranged at a private meeting to deal with the opposition by persuading conference to give them power to expel those militants who would not toe the line laid down by the Executive. The militants refused to withdraw from the position they had taken up, in favour of revolutionary political action on the class struggle basis, and the expulsions by the Executive then commenced.

One section of the militants, in Scotland, had actually formed themselves into a section of the Socialist Labour Party in 1903; accepting all that was stultifying in S.L.P. policy. This secret action was not revealed by them to the rest of the militants until 1904. The other section held a meeting in London at which it was agreed that any further attempts to bring the Social Democratic Federation in line with a genuine class struggle policy would be fruitless, and the only alternative was to form a new political organisation.

At a meeting in London on June 12th, 1904, this new organisation was formed—The Socialist Party of Great Britain.

The new party was forced into existence without premises, a party journal, literature or funds. The members immediately set about framing a Declaration of Principles and a set of rules to guide them, and also collecting funds to publish a monthly journal.

In September, 1904, the first number of the new journal, the SOCIALIST STANDARD, appeared and the editorial column contained the following statement.

> " In the past two bodies of men have put forward the claim to be Socialist parties, viz., the Independent Labour Party and the Social Democratic Federation. We who have for many years taken a share in the work of the latter organisation, and who have watched the progress of the former from its initiation, have been forced to the conclusion that through neither of them can the Social Revolution at which we aim be achieved, and that from neither of them can the working class secure redress from the ills they suffer."

This first number of the SOCIALIST STANDARD also contained the Object and Declaration of Principles that had been drawn up and agreed upon by the membership.

The last paragraph of the Principles, in particular,

was opposed to the practice of all the social democratic parties of the time, and yet the accuracy of this Principle should be obvious. There cannot be more than one Socialist party in any country because, if it *is* a genuine Socialist party, any other parties that are formed must increase the confusion in the minds of the workers and therefore retard the march to Socialism.

In spite of this obvious truth many, who claimed to be Socialists, were members of more than one organisation; some were members of the Fabian Society, the Independent Labour Party and the Social Democratic Federation, as well as, later, the Labour Party. It was their mutual adherence to reform policies that enabled members of these parties to do this without finding anything contradictory in their conduct. When the Socialist Party of Great Britain was formed its members were so conscious of this weakness that they declined to accept anybody to membership who belonged to any other political party and refused to permit its members to speak on any other political platform except in opposition.

Owing to the bitter experience of the undemocratic methods of the Social Democratic Federation the new party framed rules that gave the whole of the membership complete control of the organisation, and, in order that workers could be under no delusion about the aims and activities of the Party, all meetings, whether Branch Meetings, Executive Meetings, or Conferences, were open to the public; anyone was free to enter these meetings and listen to the discussions.

This was a revolutionary departure from custom and a severe blow to the cult of leadership, as well as eliminating any suspicion that the Party was engaged in any secret or conspiratorial activities. This policy of open meetings the Party has adhered to ever since.

Such were the circumstances that gave birth to the party that this year celebrates its fiftieth anniversary; fifty years of the consistent advocacy of Socialism without turning aside for anything.

GILMAC.

OUR PRINCIPLES STAND

Just over a hundred years ago, Marx and Engels, commenting on the drastic changes brought about by the Capitalist system of production, stated in the Communist Manifesto:—

"The bourgeoise during its rule of scarce one hundred years, has created more massive and more colossal productive forces than have all preceeding generations together. Subjection of nature's forces to man, machinery, application of chemistry to industry and agriculture, steam-navigation, railways, electric telegraphs, clearing of whole continents for cultivation, canalization of rivers, whole populations conjured out of the ground—what earlier century had even a presentiment that such productive forces slumbered in the lap of social labour?"

Since then this process has been continued at an ever increasing pace, with progressive acceleration during the past fifty years which staggers the imagination.

Even faster and more complex machinery, together with changes in technique, have brought the belt system and mass production, making the day's toil a nightmare.

Running parallel, but well to the fore, are the powers of destruction. One horror overshadows another. The high explosive and incendiary bombs of '39 are dwarfed by the Atom bomb of '45. Terrible as was the destructive power of this weapon, it has become insignificant compared with the Hydrogen bomb, making possible mass slaughter on an unpredictable scale.

Keeping pace with these abominations of destruction, and an accessory to them, is the speed of travel. Nothing is spared in human life and wealth in the mad scramble to outpace rivals in speed, an effort directed today primarily to the purpose of slaughter.

This mad world of ever more rapid changes has had its effect, among other things on the fortunes of political parties. Many that flourished fifty or less years ago are gone and almost forgotten. Others, while retaining their original names, have completely changed their character. while a few survivors are but shadows of their former selves.

The stable character of the Socialist Party of Great Britain and its consistent adherence to the principles of Socialism, stands out as an exceptional incident in the political life of this country. This fact is a fitting tribute to the ability of that small body of working men who founded the organisation and drew up its object and declaration of principles.

The clear understanding and unity of purpose which guided their action stands out in every clause of that statement. It draws a clear line of demarcation between the Socialist Party and all other political parties. It stamps the organisation as Marxist, and gives it its scientific basis. The fact that membership of the party has been conditional upon an understanding and agreement with that declaration, explains to a large extent its survival through conditions which have wrecked and destroyed so many others.

The declaration has proved invaluable as an instrument against opponents, and a sure guide in the settlement of many internal disputes. Time and time again, trained and skilled men in the art of debate, have attempted, but failed, to find a weak spot or unsound idea in it. In the conduct of Party affairs it has many times come under severe scrutiny. Often have members set out to improve that declaration, but never have they been able to propose any worth while alteration.

In internal disputes, it has proved its worth. Proposals that have run counter to it have invariably been rejected by a majority of the members, and subsequent experience has always justified their action.

In spite of the many and drastic changes which have taken place during the past fifty years, our D. of P. still stands as a clear, concise and accurate summary of the case for Socialism. This stability is to be explained by a corresponding stable feature in capitalist society, a feature which is present in all capitalist countries, no matter the form of government or degree of development. The condition is the exploitation of the wealth producers under wage slavery.

While capitalism lasts, that exploitation will continue, and until it is ended the Object and Declaration of Principles of the Party, which stem from that exploitation and are directed to its abolition, will remain valid. The problem is the same today as fifty years ago, and will remain the same until Socialism is established. The struggle between the two classes is the natural consequence of that exploitation. In its early stages it takes the form of a struggle over wages and conditions, followed with the growth of understanding, by the struggle to end exploitation.

The way this can be accomplished is dictated by the conditions of Capitalist Society. The private ownership of the means of life is the condition which enables one class to live by the exploitation of the other. The character of the means of production makes common ownership the only practical method of ending class ownership. As control is an essential part of ownership, and the only way society as a whole can control is by democratic means, we see, therefore, that the Object of the Party is dictated by the conditions of capitalism. That Object is:—

> "The establishment of a system of society based upon the common ownership and democratic control of the means and instruments for producing wealth by and in the interest of the whole community."

That is a brief definition of Socialism. It is not a scheme or an invention, but a discovery brought to light by the work of Marx and Engles in their critical examination of capitalism.

The important part the class struggle plays in the Socialist movement is self-evident. Exploitation prompts and generates the effort to secure emancipation, and emancipation to the working class can be nothing but Socialism. Socialism is, therefore, the outcome of the class struggle.

Action in conformity with this struggle, as outlined in our declaration of principles, will bring the working class to the dawn of a new social system, the potentialities of which are unbounded. Not only will it free society from the toils of class and national conflict, but will give the human race a larger measure of choice in the conduct of social affairs than it has ever experienced before.

We must not, however, allow the wonderful prospect of a classless society to blind us to the hard realities of the struggle we must face and conquer before the promised land is ours.

E. L.

OUR CONTRIBUTIONS
TO THE SOCIALIST MOVEMENT

After fifty years of the Party's existence it is worth while drawing attention to the principal contributions the Party has made to the Socialist movement.

(1). We have always insisted upon the capture of political power before any fundamental change in the social system can be accomplished.

(2). Until the majority understood and want this change Socialism cannot be achieved.

(3). Opposition to all reform policies and unswerving pursuit of Socialism as the sole objective.

(4). Opposition to all war without any distinction between alleged wars of offence, of defence, or against tyranny.

(5). The understanding that taxation is a burden upon the capitalist class and not upon the working class, and therefore any schemes which are brought forward to cut down taxes are measures of interest to the capitalist class and not to the working class.

(6). That when the workers understand their position and how to change it they will not require leaders to guide them. Leadership is the bane of the working class movement for Socialism.

(7). That Socialism is international involving the participation of workers all over the world. Therefore any suggestion of establishing Socialism in one country alone is anti-socialist.

(8). In a given country there can only be one Socialist Party, therefore no member can belong to any other political party at the same time as he is a member of the Party.

(9). Likewise no member can speak on any other political platform except in opposition.

(10). The Socialist Party must be entirely independent of all other political parties entering into no agreement or alliances for any purpose. Compromising this independence for any purpose, however seemingly innocent. will lead to non-socialists giving support to the Party.

(11). We throw our platform open to any opponent to state his case in opposition to ours.

(12). Likewise all our Executive meetings, Branch meetings and Conferences are open to the public.

(13). The members have entire control of the Party and all members are on an equal footing.

(14). Finally the Party has a scrupulous regard for political honesty and no skeletons are permitted to moulder in cupboards.

GILMAC.

THE IMPACT OF THE FIRST GREAT WAR

The 1914-1918 war had a disastrous effect upon the Party. On many Sunday mornings before the war broke out the Executive Committee had been meeting to read through and amend a pamphlet that had been drafted for publication. This had to be abandoned and the pamphlet was not considered again until a few years after the war ended. Another project that had to be abandoned was the appointment of a paid Secretary-Organiser. Money had been subscribed for this purpose, the member selected, the Executive Committee were discussing the date when he should start and the work he should start upon when the war put an end to the idea.

The war dealt its worst blow to the membership. The Military Service Act, which came into operation in March, 1916, applied immediately to a large body of active young members and, eventually, to nearly all the men in the Party. The Appeal Tribunals that were set up were quite useless, as far as members were concerned, and were treated by them largely as a means to put the Party's case where possible; generally, however, the objections of members only got a few minutes hearing. In order to escape the clutches of the authorities many members " disappeared " and some we never saw again; others went to prison.

Immediately the war broke out we drew up a Manifesto which was published in the September 1914 SOCIALIST STANDARD; the August number was already printed. This Manifesto is reprinted in our pamphlet on War. In the same September issue of the SOCIALIST STANDARD an editorial article appeared setting out the real basis of the conflict and concluding with the following paragraph:—

" The question for the working class, then, is not that of British or German victory, since either event will leave them wage-slaves living upon wages. Under German rule those wages cannot be reduced lower than under British, for every British working man knows that the masters who are shouting so loudly today for us to go and die in defence of our shackles and their shekels, have left no stone unturned to force wages to the lowest possible limits. The question, then, before the workers, is the abolition of the whole social system of which war and unemployment are integral parts, and the establishment of society upon the basis of common ownership of the means of production—the establishment, that is, of Socialism."

The Executive Commitee passed a resolution stating that any member who voluntarily joined the fighting forces was unfit for membership of a Socialist Party. This attitude the members loyally adhered to during the course of the war.

Outdoor speaking during the war was extremely difficult. There were many turbulent meetings. Some meetings were broken up and members had to defend the speaker and the platform. Speakers were arrested for " spreading disaffection amongst His Majesty's subjects." A speaker was arrested at Leicester and followed to the police station by a crowd howling for his blood. He was released, after a week, on giving an undertaking not to appear on the platform again for six months. When he got back to London he phoned his employers intending to give a plausible reason for his absence. He did not get that far. He was told his wages would be sent on and they never wanted to see him again. Later he learned that one of his fellow clerks had obligingly pinned up a report of his case in the manager's office.

One instance in particular reflected the attitude of the authorities towards our speakers. One of them got upon the platform and, before putting our case, said he would read to the audience Lord Roberts' Circular to Commanding Officers in India. Before he got half way through the circular the police intervened and took him off to the police station where he was charged with "spreading disaffection." When he came before the magistrate he protested that he had made no personal contribution at all; that he was arrested whilst in the middle of reading Lord Roberts' circular. The magistrate asked to see the circular and, after reading it, said " Well there is nothing wrong with the circular, but, read at a meeting in the present circumstances, it was likely to cause disaffection amongst His Majesty's subjects." He then warned the speaker not to repeat his crime and fined him £2 2s. . . . As a matter of interest the circular dealt in detail with the selection and care of native girls to act as prostitutes for the soldiers in India under official licence !

The difficulties of speaking increased so much that a Party meeting was called to decide whether it was worth while continuing. A majority decided that it was not. On the front page of January 1915 SOCIALIST STANDARD we informed readers of our decision to suspend outdoor propaganda and the reasons that forced us to this decision. The article, in large type, appeared under the heading " Under Martial Law."

So outdoor meetings were closed down but the columns of the S.S. continued to criticise all concerned in the war and to put the Socialist attitude on the war. Every issue was full of statements that came under the Regulations and members were expecting the Head Office to be raided and the Party compulsorily closed down. In October 1916 the War Office informed us that the *S.S.* was prohibited from being sent outside the United Kingdom on the ground that a portion of its contents " might be used by the enemy powers for their propaganda." In 1917 the Head Office was raided by the police but there was nothing left there to interest them; all Party records had been deposited elsewhere and the General Secretary at the time, Hilda Kohn, carried the current minute book around in her bag.

During the war the funds of the Party got very low and an urgent call for donations brought in very little. But the members who were left managed to hold out until the end, although we had to give up our premises in 1918 and move to a couple of rooms on the first floor of a house behind Oxford Street.

When the war ended members began to drift back and the job of rebuilding the Party was commenced with enthusiasm and success.

GILMAC.

THE RUSSIAN REVOLUTION

Its impact on the Socialist Movement

When the Russian Revolution broke upon war-weary Europe in 1917 most of the present members of the Socialist Party of Great Britain were either unborn or very young. To most of us the Russian Revolution is past history, as indeed it is to most people living to-day.

Whilst a knowledge of events relatively so recent is easy to acquire, the emotional impact of those events on politically-minded working men and women in this country, reformist and self-styled revolutionary alike, is harder to recapture. The fervour aroused by this impact even seeped into the S.P.G.B. Growing up into manhood in the years following the first world war, it is difficult for any young politically-interested worker, unbriefed in Socialist theory, to escape the influence of the emotionalism and the fervour which clouded opinion on the happenings in Russia. The Socialist revolution had started in Russia and would sweep through Europe! The workers would rise (at the psychological moment), form their own councils (Soviets) and take over the land, the mines and the factories. Parliament had been shown by the events in Russia to be " useless "—a " gas house." Every strike was interpreted by the new, self-appointed, Bolshevik theorists in this country as a move in the strategy of the coming struggle for Socialism. Those who seemed quite unaware of this development were the workers generally, though the English Bolsheviks seemed not to notice the fact.

One result of the Russian Revolution was the formation of the British Communist Party in 1920. The Socialist Labour Party, an organisation formed in 1903 and allegedly Marxist, split and some of its prominent members became leaders of the new organisation, which devoted itself to preparing for the " psychological moment." So seriously did it take this mumbo-jumbo that at one time in the late twenties Communists wrote to the S.P.G.B. declining a challenge to debate on the grounds that there was not time to debate Socialism—" it was round the corner." Others who joined the early Commu-

nist Party came from the I.L.P. and the Labour Party, it being possible at that time to be a member of each party at one and the same time, the assumption being that the different branches of the " working class movement " were moving towards the same goal even if " tactics " differed. Even one or two members of the S.P.G.B. found their way into the Communist Party.

As a political party, however, the Socialist Party remained unshaken in its basic attitudes by the events in Russia. It would be an understatement to say that the Socialist Party shewed a disinclination to identify itself with the " working-class movement " on Russian questions. Whilst not unmoved by the events in Russia we rejected what Communists claimed were the lessons to be applied from it to England. We saw nothing in the Russian upheaval which would make it necessary for the Party to deviate from the course it has set itself at its foundation in 1904. We rejected the propositions that a Socialist revolution had taken place in Russia, that the working class had come to power, that " intellectual minorities " could " lead " an unprepared working class to Socialism, that Parliament was " useless " and that Russia had forged new instruments for working class emancipation. We expressed our views forcefully and objectively on these issues which resulted in bitter opposition from our opponents, as the SOCIALIST STANDARD and propagandists of twenty and more years ago testify. Our attitude on the Russian question is unchanged to-day and there is nothing that was written by our comrades in 1918 about it that we would withdraw. In contrast, prominent members of the Labour Party, who, whilst making pious reservations about the " violent methods " of the Bolsheviks in the early years, expressed approval of their aims and thought Russia was Socialist; but to-day see Russia as an empire-building, police state. It is an odd thought what the next thirty years might bring when one reflects that early Communist M.P.s like Newbold and Saklatvala owed their seats in Parliament to the fact that they were candidates of the Labour Party whilst at the same time being members of the Communist Party. Time and events have brought changes of attitudes among erstwhile supporters of the Bolsheviks. Having little or no theoretical knowledge, support, idolatry and tolerance have given way to criticism and bitter opposition. The Socialist Party of Great Britain opposed the basic assumptions of the Bolsheviks and their English supporters as unsound and non-Marxist, and the consequent development of affairs in Russia since the Revolution has occasioned us no surprise.

Without reservation the Socialist Party refuted the claim that the Bolsheviks could introduce Socialism in Russia. We were critical of their aims and methods. Socialism was impossible before large scale, industrial production had developed, and with it also, a dispossessed working class population had been formed and won over to Socialism. The position in Russia was that it was a country largely populated by a peasantry, dominated by a semi-feudal aristocracy. Capitalist production was small in relation to the economy as a whole. Politically, the land-owning aristocracy were dominant and in control, the capitalist class were weak and insignificant, the working class was relatively numerically small though its organisations were semi-insurrectionary, vigorous and well organised. Parliamentary government in the *Duma* was a facade and creaked under the burden of aristocratic privilege and power: the franchise made a mockery of democracy.

Unable to deal with the complex problems thrown up by the war, the Russian Imperial Government, in 1917, began to lose authority and prestige. Lack of transport, food and arms, led to seething discontent among the soldiers, workers and peasants. It was in these circumstances that the Soviets (loosely organised councils or committees) established themselves among the workers, the soldiers and the peasants. The weaker and the more incompetent the Government were to control the situation the stronger the Soviets became and the more authority they assumed. The tottering Imperial government gave way in March, 1917, to the Kerensky regime. Kerensky was leader of the Mensheviks, who were, like the Bolsheviks, a section of the Social Democratic Party. The Kerensky regime lasted until November, 1917. Its failure resulted from its complete inability to assess the widespread discontent with the war among the soldiers, workers and peasants. Where the Mensheviks failed the Bolsheviks succeeded. They realistically exploited these discontents in the meetings of the Soviets. As the authority of the new regime declined so the Bolsheviks gained in popularity in the Soviets and the prestige of the Soviets grew. There were instances of some constitutional powers passing from the government to the Soviets. The slogan of the Bolsheviks became " All Power to the Soviets " and " Peace, Land and Bread." They crystallised the discontents and spread rapidly throughout Russia. The Kerensky regime, following its corrupt predecessor, came to its end.

The Bolsheviks had come to power in Russia. The Soviets, despite their spontaneous and improvised character had assumed constitutional forms and power. Amid all the excitements and the interest in the Russian Revolution aroused outside Russia the S.P.G.B. remained calm. From the outset it knew it could repudiate the wild claims that were being made. Whatever the merit of the slogan and

object of " Peace, Land and Bread," we said, this was not Socialism, and that, in the absence of knowledge and understanding among the majority of the population, could not lead to it. Further, we argued, this knowledge and understanding could not arise in the absence of maturity in productive relations and social development. Any government which assumed power in such circumstances, whether it claimed to be Socialist or not, must make itself responsible for the problems of capitalism and bring upon itself the opposition of the workers—they must fail. We were right.

In 1917 the Bolsheviks kept an earlier promise in arranging for free elections to a Constituent Assembly. When the result of the elections showed a majority opposed to the Bolsheviks, the government of the latter, which controlled the armed forces through the Soviets, decisively suppressed it. That was one of its first openly terroristic acts. It was certainly not the last. What idealism, principles or Socialist ideas might have existed in the pre-1917 Bolshevik movement in Russia, soon became lost in the evolution of the autocratic tyranny that soon established itself and remains firmly in the saddle to-day.

If there are lessons to be learned from Russia and other parts of the world where capitalism is administered in the name of Socialism and by men who sprang from the workers it is that the only way to Socialism is through working class understanding and democracy.

H. W.

WORDS, WORDS, WORDS . . .

"I am told that people say I bawl. Well, I allow it, I *do* bawl and I *will* bawl." So said a famous tub-thumper of two hundred years ago, and in various tones, for various causes, they—we—have been bawling ever since.

Rhetoric under the sky is the oldest, most powerful form of persuasion. It was done in the agora, the market place that was the centre of social and political life in a Greek city. Petronius heckled an orator in Nero's Rome —" by a set of dribbling witticisms you found you could make audiences titter "—on his way to the bawdyhouse. In mediæval England John Ball stood on hillsides demanding freedom and justice for the poor. In Shakespeare's day news, scandal and sedition were put into ballads and sung in the markets, and old Saint Paul's was " the market of young lecturers, whom you may cheapen here at all rates and sizes "; Mark Antony—and his audience—had their prototypes. Through the centuries that followed, in the squares and open spaces they cried salvation and the rights of man—the revivalists, the Chartists and the rest.

The Socialist Party was founded when open-air meetings had never been more copious, when the sects and parties vied with one another in the streets for the attention of the working class. Different conditions engender different approaches. There was more rhetoric in those days —to the modern mind more " ham " perhaps, but it was necessary. The slick, confidence-making political speech belonged to the wireless-telegraph future. Aspiring speakers, practising declamation, tried " The Charge of the Light Brigade ", " Men of England " and " The Bells " on one another.

Politically conscious people were more theory-conscious than they are to-day. Marx and Engels were not long dead, Kautsky, Luxemburg and Plechanov in their prime; Bernstein's revisionism and the Fabian Essays were argued fiercely. Socialist speakers had to know their theory and know it well. Many of them learned by heart what were considered key passages of important works: sections of *The Communist Manifesto*, the statement of historical materialism from *The Critique of Political Economy*, pages of *Capital*, of Darwin, Spencer and *No Compromise*, and bits of Shakespeare too. It was a fine thing to support the analysis of capitalism with

"... You take my life

When you do take the means whereby I live."

If the politicos were more learned, the others made up for it. A speaker too vigorous in attacking the prejudices of a prejudiced audience was asking to be thrown in a horse-trough, and not uncommonly he was. Robert Tressell describes the reception of a " Clarion " van by the ragged-trousered philanthropists of Hastings:

"The man on the platform was still trying to make himself heard, but without success. The strangers who had come with the van and the little group of local socialists, who had forced their way close to the platform in front of the would-be speaker, only increased the din by their shouts of appealing to the crowd to ' give the man a fair chance.' This little bodyguard closed round the van as it began to move slowly downhill, but it was completely outnumbered. . . ' We'll give the swines Socialism!' shouted Crass, who was literally foaming at the mouth."

On most platforms, feeling carried the day. The Liberals and Tories could raise cheers with reference to the Empire and the Flag; the worst accusation against a policy was " it will ruin the country". Emotion was not altogether disfavoured by Socialists. Words like " traitor " carried a great deal; labour leaders were invariably called " Labour bleeders " or " fakirs ", and there was even a Party song called " The World for the Workers ".

The platform manner changed after the first war, at the same time as urban growth and road traffic began to eliminate meeting-places. The radio and the pictures arrived, and speakers had to compete with them. Some of the smaller parties were swallowed by the Labour and Communist Parties, so that theoretical argument gave place to " practical policies " and calls for " action now." In the 'thirties a new sort of political meeting appeared, with the speaker surrounded by microphones and no questions allowed. The rhetorical tradition of Parliament, too, suffered a blow when Labour came to power with Cabinet Ministers who were without oral grace; Gladstone, Balfour and their contemporaries could often be taken down verbatim to read as excellent prose.

Today audiences are more tolerant (and more knowledgeable too) and speakers, on the whole, more urbane and more discursive. Perhaps there are more wisecracks and fewer long quotations, because our age prefers the former as a condiment to learning. One tradition which the Party has always maintained is that of giving the platform to opposition. Other parties don't do it; the Socialist Party, which has everything to gain and nothing to fear from open discussion, never refuses, and many a truculent opponent has deflated himself trying to present a case against Socialism under the Socialist Party's own auspices.

The industriousness of Party speakers has always been remarkable. Before the first war, two dozen of them held something like a hundred and thirty open-air meetings a month in London alone. The numbers were similar in 1939, and today the meetings still are a vital part of the Party's propaganda. Debates, too: Liberals, Labour,

Tories, Communists, pacifists, fascists, parsons, anarchists —all of them have had their petty panaceas atomized by Socialist speakers. Several debates were published as pamphlets, and they are remarkable examples of the Party's case in action.

Fifty years' speaking for Socialism—fifty years of writing for it, as well. The SOCIALIST STANDARD is unique. It has never known a paid journalist; its writers and editors have been bricklayers, clerks, housewives, busmen—all sorts and conditions of working people in their spare time. The first page of the first issue said:

> "In the Socialist Party of Great Britain we are all members of the working class, and cannot hope that our articles will always be finely phrased, but we shall endeavour to lay before you on every occasion a sane and sound pronouncement on all matters affecting the welfare of the working class. What we lack in refinement of style we shall make good by the depth of our sincerity and by the truth of our principles."

The STANDARD was too hard-hitting to have much refinement, and there was little room for fine phrases in Fitzgerald's relentless logic or the rumbustious onslaughts of Jacomb. Euphemism was scorned, and the contributors said just what they meant. When the *Manchester Guardian* slighted the Party, a STANDARD headline called it the "Liberal skunk press"; Lloyd George was a liar, Asquith an assassin, and their confreres hypocrites, frauds and political prostitutes. It seems surprising that the Party was sued for libel only once.

The style of the STANDARD then, as now, owed to two principal sources: the sociological textbooks of the time, and popular journalism. From the latter it drew a peculiar Joe Miller waggishness that was part of the stock-in-trade of successful newspaper columnists, easier to exemplify than describe. Thus, the Editorial Committee apologizing for a writer who had not made himself clear to a correspondent: "He developed what he calls his style by studying a burr-walnut piano case in foggy weather". A debate with a suffragette was irresistible, and its report was resplendent with quips about "ye gallant knight Anderson" and "the poor girl". Perhaps the acme of this sort of wit was with a highly dramatic poem which had the refrain:

> "Go! reckon your dead by your forges red,
>   And in factories where we spin;
> If blood be the price of your cursed wealth,
>   By Christ! we have paid in full".

The poem was called "Gawd Struth We Have."

The writers on economics, socialist theory and political issues put forth their subject-matter lucidly and without frills or ambiguities; style which came naturally through close acquaintance with Engels, Kautsky, Plechanov and the other classical exponents of Marxism. The popularization of academic and technical subjects influenced later writers, and is still doing so—"science for the citizen" has made its mark. Just as on the platform, the people addressed are more widely informed and less concerned with theoretical questions. That does not mean, however, that the modern writer—or speaker—may neglect theory; it means that he must apply it more widely in a world with wider horizons.

And so it goes on; the business of persuading people to think straight, because that is what the Socialist wants. Words are our weapons. Words, words, words . . .

R. COSTER.

THOSE

WERE

THE DAYS

Even in those far-off days Paddington was a very active branch. They had amongst them five official speakers, two chairmen, two members of the E.C—one of whom edited the S.S. for a time—and two writers. And— there was a choir. About ten musically minded members used to foregather at a member's house before Branch Meeting and blend their voices in what it was hoped was harmony. It was, in any case, very enjoyable. One Christmas Eve it was suggested we go carol singing for Party funds. A carol is defined as a religious song in praise of Christmas; but the dictionary also says that to carol is to warble. So we went warbling. In view of our object, where better we reasoned than bourgeois Bayswater!

It was a beautiful evening, as like as could be, one of the more popular Christmas cards; keen, bright, a powdering of snow but dry underfoot and a pale moon overhead. Sedate Bayswater was very peaceful, and it was with an almost guilty feeling we shattered the silence with "Hail Smiling Morn." Further items from our repertoire followed and presently a butler emerged to bestow upon our efforts his blessing and a shilling. Another pitch drew blank, but a few further successes encouraged us to keep going. Then came the reveller. A hansom cab drew up and discharged—discharged is the word—a festive figure complete with tall hat, opera-cloak, a roll of music and a load of alcohol. He insisted on beating time with his music roll to the strains of "Brightly Dawns our Wedding-day," and to "Comrades-in-Arms." "Hail Smiling Morn" incited him to dance, but alcohol did not aid his agility, and after degenerating into an elephantine shuffle, he bestowed upon us his blessing and half-a-crown. A further half-crown—quite a sum in those days—came from a window, thrown to us by a smiling housemaid. After that a financial famine seemed to set in and a friendly butler explained to us that Bayswater was empty except for servants; all the families had gone to the country for Christmas. We should have guessed it. However, we enjoyed the experience and Party funds benefited—if memory serves—by about 12/6.

W. T. H.

A. KOHN

Kohn became interested in politics when very young, taking part in discussions at Marble Arch, Hyde Park, when only a youth. In 1908 he joined the Party and was soon very active as a writer and speaker; he spoke on the outdoor platform nearly every evening for some years.

Soon after joining the party he started a private book agency and was the principal means of bringing English translations of foreign Socialist classics to many of us at a time when they were little known in England.

Practically all his life Socialism and books were his main interests. He read voraciously and few had his knowledge of books, past and present, on different aspects of the working-class movement. He was a forceful and humorous speaker, both indoor and outdoor, and early in the 1914 war he had some rowdy meetings. At one of his meetings in 1914 at Marble Arch the crowd rushed the platform, after a hectic meeting, and the police had to escort him through an angry crowd of " patriots " and across the road to the tube station.

During 1915, when the passing of the Conscription Act became certain, Kohn left for America, where he remained for about six years and made many friends in Canada and the U.S.A. While out there he wrote and spoke on Socialism and also organised classes. He sent articles to the SOCIALIST STANDARD from America, and the last one, in 1917, was picked up by the American authorities, who took exception to its anti-war contents and made considerable efforts to trace him. They also pressed the English authorities for assistance, and the latter called Fitzgerald up for questioning and kept him in a cell for a night. They also had his sister along at Scotland Yard for interrogation. However, they never traced Kohn and the matter was eventually dropped.

Arising out of the above police investigation there were two humourous incidents, which it seems to the present writer are worth recording. Fitzgerald was very methodical and also extremely critical of members whose " stupidity " helped the authorities to collect members whose military position was doubtful. When Fitzgerald was arrested and searched the police found in his pocket his address book, which contained the addresses of most of us! The other incident concerned Kohn's sister. Although she was secretary of the Party at the time, the police failed to discover that she was even a member of the Party.

Kohn was on the Executive Committee and the Editorial Committee before 1914, and he was again on the Editorial Committee from 1924 to 1929. He wrote many excellent articles for the SOCIALIST STANDARD and was by nature very lively, full of jokes, and fond of company. Even when he was dying, humour still stirred in him.

A little while before the second world war his health broke down, and in 1940 he had to go into hospital for treatment. While there the hospital was hit by a bomb, and a few weeks later the room where he lodged was badly blasted. After a couple of years out of hospital, T.B. developed, and early in 1944 he was back in hospital again, where he remained until his death on the 28th December, 1944. He was twice evacuated on account of the hospital being hit by flying bombs, finally reaching the temporary hospital quarters in a large house in North Wales where he died at the age of 56.

Kohn's brain was crammed with knowledge of the international working-class movement, and he was intellectually generous to members and sympathisers—always ready to answer a question or explain a point. He gave almost the whole of his life to the struggle for Socialism.

GILMAC.

THE GENERAL STRIKE

The year 1926 was a most momentous one in working class history. It was the year of the greatest battle ever fought by the British trade union movement—the general strike.

The great world war of 1914-1918 created a vacuum in the world's markets and during the trade boom that followed British workers were able to wring a few concessions from their employers. As markets again became saturated with goods and trade declined, the tables were turned and the employers launched an attack to reduce wages and depress conditions of work.

The reparation terms imposed upon Germany after the war caused German coal to be diverted to markets that had previously been the prerogative of British coal traders. This aggravated the slump in the British coal industry and the wages and working hours of coal miners became the prime target when the employers took the offensive. In 1925, when their wages were already reduced to miserable limits, the miners were threatened with a further wage reduction, extension of their hours of work and the break-up of their national negotiating machinery.

The Miners' Federation of Great Britain rejected the employers' demands and received the support of the Trade Union Congress General Council which arranged with the railway and transport unions for united action. The employers, lined up behind the Government, were unprepared for such action and beat a hasty retreat. The day the coal owners withdrew their demands passed into history as Red Friday.

The trade unions were jubilant but the employers and the Government set to work making detailed preparations for the show-down that they intended to bring about. A few trade unionists, like Mr. A. J. Cook, the Miners' Secretary, realised that only the first round had been fought and they called for preparations for the next struggle, but nothing was done.

Meanwhile, an Organisation for the Maintenance of Supplies (O.M.S.) was set up under the control of a number of military and naval commanders and prominent capitalists, whilst the Government stalled off the trade unions with a Royal Commission, under the chairmanship of Sir Herbert Samuel, to inquire into the coal industry.

When the Samuel Report was issued in March, 1926, it was specific only in its assertions that the miners should accept lower pay and longer hours. Some members of the General Council of the T.U.C. argued that the miners should accept the terms of the Commission's report pending a reorganisation of the coal industry that the report recommended, but the miners adopted a slogan, "Not a penny off the pay, not a second on the day."

The General Council of the T.U.C. entered into negotiations with the Government, trying by all means, even "almost grovelling" as Mr. J. H. Thomas, of the National Union of Railwaymen admitted, to find a way to divert the head-on crash that was ahead. Finally, Mr. Baldwin the Prime Minister, turned his back on the workers' leaders and refused further negotiations on the grounds that a general strike was threatened and that certain overt acts had already taken place, including gross interference with the freedom of the Press. This referred to the action of certain printers who had refused to print some anti-working class statements. The fight was on.

On Friday, April 30th, the King signed a Proclamation declaring a State of Emergency. Orders in Council were issued in the form of Emergency Regulations under the Emergency Powers Act. Local Authorities were reminded by a Ministry circular of the measures that had been previously arranged to cope with a national stoppage. Troops were moved to South Wales, Lancashire and Scotland and arrangements made to call in the Navy. The O.M.S. placarded the country with a poster calling for recruits.

On the third of May the General Council of the T.U.C. issued a manifesto and the following day the General Strike commenced. The stoppage exceeded expectations. All workers called upon responded magnificently, as did many who were not called upon. There were no evening papers and no passenger trains. All army leave was cancelled and the Government took over the B.B.C.

At midnight the taxi drivers came out and the next day saw seamen, transport workers, printers, journalists, engineers, dockers and many others all solidly on strike. The Government took over the *Morning Post* and issued the official *British Gazete* under the editorship of Mr. Churchill, whilst the T.U.C. took over the *Daily Herald* and published *The British Worker*.

By the third day of the strike 82 unions were involved and, considering the lack of preliminary preparation, the workers' organisation was splendid. Each succeeding day more and more workers joined the strike and the Government took further action including the formation of a "Civil Constabulary Reserve," composed of ex-soldiers with wages higher than those paid to miners. On the eighth day the High Court of Justice declared the strike illegal. The Government prepared to confiscate money sent by overseas trade unions to help their striking colleagues in Britain. The B.B.C. announced "There is as yet little sign of a collapse of the strike." There was no rowdyism, and clashes with the police and other authorities were of a minor nature.

At midday on the ninth day the General Council of the T.U.C. arrived at Downing Street and informed the Prime Minister that the General Strike was being terminated that day and the news was broadcast at 1 p.m. followed by the publication of an order by the General Council for a cessation of the strike. Sir Herbert Samuel had issued a personal unauthorative memorandum to the members of the council and they had seized upon it as an excuse to call off the strike. The miners were left to carry on an heroic struggle on their own till they succumbed in December, not even having been notified of the intending surrender.

Throughout the strike the General Council closed its eyes to the class conflict in which it was involved and insisted that the issue was purely an industrial one. Not so the Government. It realised clearly the class character of its own acts and called for support from the un-class conscious by addressing them as " the nation " and telling them that Parliament and the constitution were threatened.

The Labour Party acted and spoke similarly to the General Council of the T.U.C. It blamed the Government but did not want to see the Government defeated. Hypocritically, it said that had it been in office it would have avoided such a situation, conveniently forgetting that only two years earlier it had been prepared to evoke the Emergency Powers Act in similar circumstances when it was faced with a transport strike.

The Communists went wild and were responsible for many of the clashes with the police. They cried that Parliament was finished and demanded all power to the General Council. They saw a revolution every time a lorry was overturned or a policeman lost his helmet. After the strike they laid the blame for the capitulation to the cowardice of the members of the General Council and demanded the replacement of the cowards.

It is not easy to analyse an event immediately it has taken place, yet, such is the nature of Socialist analysis, that we would not amend one paragraph, alter one sentence or delete one word of what the Socialist Party of Great Britain said about the General Strike at the time. The twenty-eight years that have elapsed have only served to confirm what our comrades of those days wrote in the SOCIALIST STANDARD.

The two outstanding lessons of the General Strike were, firstly, that while political power is in the hands of the capitalist class, and until such time as the workers take it into their own hands, they must expect defeat in industrial struggles that threaten the interests of the whole capitalist class. Secondly, the evils of leadership. To blame the General Council or call them cowards and traitors solves nothing. To replace them by other leaders is merely to invite continuous repetitions of similar debacles. To be free of cowards, traitors, hypocrites, fakirs, and even well intentioned mis-leaders, the workers must see to it that their representatives are their servants, not their masters, carrying out instructions, not giving them.

When the workers are prepared to put as much effort and heroism into the struggle for Socialism as they were prepared to devote in support of the striking miners in 1926, there will be a grand story to tell.

W. WATERS.

OUR MANY HEAD OFFICES

Our Party has had a number of Head Offices in the course of its career. Until recently most of them have been fair reflections of our slender funds.

Our first Head Office was little more than an address: The Communist Club, 107, Charlotte Street, W.1. Then in 1905 we rented a room for certain evenings at 1A, Caledonian Road, King's Cross Road. Here the Executive Committee used to meet on alternate Saturdays and Thursdays. Then in 1906 we rented a room at 28, Cursitor Street, where, for the first time the Executive Committee met every Tuesday evening. After some trouble with the landlord we took a room at 22, Great James Street, just off Theobalds Road, in 1907.

In 1909 we began really to move upward. We got two rooms on the first floor of a house in 10, Sandland Street, Bedford Row (a little behind the north side of Holborn). This was the first Head Office visited by the present writer. When he went there as a youth he felt he had really reached the heart of deep red revolution. The ground floor was an old dilapidated junk shop. The side door led up two flights of dark rickety stairs to a couple of bare rooms. The floor was bare boards.. One room contained an old desk for the use of the General Secretary and anyone else who had writing to do. Beside was piled the stock of unsold STANDARDS. As time passed the pile grew far beyond the height of the desk until it was in danger of being knocked down by anyone passing. The other room contained a long table and some chairs. This room was used for economics classes on Thursday evenings and for folding STANDARDS on Saturdays On Tuesday evenings the table was moved into the secretarial room for the E.C. meetings. When the E.C. was sitting it was almost impossible to get anyone else into the room, in spite of the fact that we advertised and boasted that our E.C. meetings were open to the public—so they were, if you could get in!

While we were at Sandland Street the General Secretary, Sammy Quelch, had a coffee shop nearby, and he had a habit of pinning a note on the door asking any members who called to go round to the coffee shop. Robert Blatchford had a humorous dig at the Party in his paper

The Clarion (the most popular Labour paper of its day) at the time. He said he "called at the Headquarters of the Socialist Party of Great Britain but found that the Party had gone to get a cup of coffee." Later this was changed to "The Secretary, the Treasurer, and the member had gone to get a cup of coffee."

The old junk shop was bombed during the last war and it and the adjoining houses completely obliterated. But the fire, passion and enthusiasm of the members that gathered in those two bleak rooms above the shop still lingers in the memory. There was a tough old member without arms (he had lost them in an accident in Africa) who used to sell boot laces and matches and would come in breathless and dripping with rain to tell of a meeting that was being held so that members could hurry there with literature to sell. He was one of the best literature sellers the Party had and was active for many years. Later on he surmounted his difficulties sufficiently to earn a comfortable living. His name was Germain.

Head Office was moved from Sandland Street to 193, Grays Inn Road in 1912. There we had two ground floor rooms and a basement in which, for the first time, the literature was put into proper order. One of the members, T. W. Lobb, made curved seats that ran round the walls of the front room. This room was large enough for the E.C. to sit round the table on chairs whilst visitors could sit along the walls.

Next door was a rather poor coffee shop but the owner had a sympathy for us and helped us in many ways, particularly during the first Great War. Every Saturday he would come in with cloths and a pail of water and clean the windows. When the police were waiting to raid us he gave the secretary word of the two men he saw watching our place and enabled her to direct E.C. members into his shop to decide what to do about holding their meetings.

The first war broke out whilst we were at Grays Inn Road, and it was there that the War Manifesto was prepared and members met to decide upon the course of action to meet the various difficulties arising out of that calamitous event. The times were certainly stirring as the pages of the SOCIALIST STANDARD during those devastating years will reveal.

During the six years we were at Grays Inn Road a great deal of work was done. Before the war preparations were completed for putting a paid Organising Secretary into the field; economics and other classes and discussions were held regularly; members would meet to decide about making visits to outlying places to hold impromptu meetings; and a host of other plans were made and accomplished. Someone managed to buy an old printing machine on which leaflets, E.C. reports and treasurer's reports were printed. Comrade Alley, who recently passed away, used to set them up in type and leave a note for members to run them off—very laboriously by swinging a long arm across.

In 1918 we were forced to leave Grays Inn Road and we took two rooms on the first floor of a house at 28, Union Street, W.1, just behind Oxford Street. There again the people in the shop below were sympathetic. It was a sweet shop and if any dubious caller made an appearance or there was any urgent message one of the price-cards in the window would be turned upside-down. The General Secretary at that time occupied the floor above Head Office.

These rooms were only a temporary refuge. The next year, 1919, we got premises at 17, Mount Pleasant, opposite the G.P.O. Sorting Office. We had two floors and a fair-sized basement. It was the most "respectable" Head Office we had had up to that time, and we remained there eight years. It was to this office that many wandering members returned after the war. One night, soon after we had taken up occupation, a powerful voice outside roared a greeting to a member and then Moses Baritz walked in. He was back after being released from prison in America where he had been interned for his anti-war activities. When he went out to America during the war his hair was coal black; when he returned it was snow-white. Prison had been torment to a man of his nervous energy.

Several Australian seamen visited us at this office in the Twenties. Some of them later took part in forming our companion party in Australia. We also had visitors from America who helped to form our companion party in the United States.

In 1927 Fitzgerald, with the aid of map and compass, succeeded in proving to a majority of the E.C. members that the Elephant and Castle was really in the centre of London. Anyhow we moved over near there to 42, Great Dover Street. We took an old house with three floors and a basement. One of the members made fittings for keeping the *S.S.* and literature in proper order in one basement room. The other basement room (a very small one) had tables and chairs, and a stove on which a woman member cooked for those who wanted a meal. The smoke and heat in the little place was stifling, and getting out when one had finished was a problem.

The ground floor front room was used for selling literature and packing. There was a small shop front in which literature was displayed. The first floor consisted of one good sized room in which meetings were held as well as an occasional social—when the place shook as if it was about to collapse. E.C. meetings were also held in this room. Here we had some interesting discussions on the Spanish Revolt and at the beginning of the last war. In the room above lectures were given on many subjects during the winter months.

In April 1941 a bomb fell on this house destroying most of our stuff and we had to get temporary premises at 33, Gloucester Place, which consisted of two ground floor rooms. In April, 1943, we took over Rugby Chambers, Rugby Street, just off Theobalds Road.. These premises had been occupied by the Electrical Trades Union. It was from here that we ran our first Parliamentary candidate in 1945. It was also while we were here that the Party membership began to expand and the funds to reach reasonable proportions. With greater activity, the need for more space and increasing rent the members looked round for more suitable premises. A fund was started and sufficient money donated by members and friends to enable us to buy our present premises at 52, Clapham High Street, which we took over in March, 1951. Here at last we have a place of our own, with a small hall for meetings, and suitable accommodation for the secretary, committee, a library, a canteen, and a room in which members can meet and discuss.

After many ups and downs it looks as if we have reached a settled place at last.

GILMAC.

OUR ELECTORAL ACTIVITIES

The Socialist Party, owing to lack of means, are unable to put up candidates this election, but every voter who adheres to Socialist principles, may vote for Socialism by writing the word Socialism across his or her ballot paper as shown above. To do this is to register a demand for a Socialist candidate.

(*Reproduced from front page of* SOCIALIST STANDARD *December,* 1918.)

One of my cherished papers is an Election Manifesto dated the first of November 1906 entitled Battersea Borough Council Election, Latchmere Ward; underneath this title are the words, Battersea Branch of the Socialist Party of Great Britain, followed by the object of the Party, and at the bottom of the front page, the words Socialist candidates' Election Address. Inside is an article, addressed to the Electors of Latchmere Ward, which explained the struggle for political supremacy, the necessity for class organisation, and exposed Municipalism (a now forgotten issue). The bogey of the rates was dealt with, the article ending as follows: " The Socialist Party of Great Britain therefore enters into municipal contests as a step in the work of capturing the whole of the political machinery. Fully realising and pointing out to workers the strict limitations of the power of local bodies, making no promises that are beyond our power to fulfil, we ask the members of our class, when (but not before) they have studied these facts, and realise their correctness, to cast their vote for the candidates of the S.P.G.B., who alone stand on the above basis".

Finally appear the candidates names, George Frederich Moody, Frank Craske, George Money.

This was the first Election Manifesto issued by the Party, and is a reprint from the front page article in the October 1906 issue of the SOCIALIST STANDARD.

It was also used in the other Wards, at Battersea, and the Tooting Ward of Wandsworth.

There were twelve candidates put forward, at the 1906 municipal Elections, nine in Battersea and three in Wandsworth. The Battersea results were Latchmere Ward, Craske 117, Moody 117, Money 113. Winstanley Ward, Blewett 57, Roe 49, Witcher 45. Church Ward, Greenham 93, Fawcett 88, Hunt 77 (incidentally Comrade Roe is still with us, and was a delegate for his branch at the 1954 Conference). At Wandsworth Tooting Ward, it was Barker 94, MacManus 77, Dumenil 59; of these votes fifty were for our candidates alone.

The SOCIALIST STANDARD for December 1906 commented :—" All the candidates fought on the Election Manifesto published in our October issue, a few were distributed in each Ward. They had no programme of ear-tickling, side tracking, vote-catching "paliatives" and did no canvassing. The candidates were practically unknown and had not climbed into popularity on the backs of the working class, by posing as 'leaders' of unemployed deputations 'right to live' councils, and similar confusionist conglomerations".

Arising out of these Battersea contests, the question of non members signing nomination papers for candidates, was raised. The Executive Committee ruled that in future only Party members should sign nomination forms, which was later embodied in Party Rules.

The opening paragraphs of the election leaflet for the general election of this year was as follows:—

"Fellow members of the Working Class! at the present moment you, or those of you possessed of votes, are being urgently reminded of a fact that you may be pardoned for having forgotten—you are of consequence; then you, who but yesterday were 'hands,' dependant, hirelings, articles of merchandise are today dictators, history-makers, freemen, you are the power in the State. You hold the destiny of the Empire in the hollow of your hand. Yesterday, those of you who were unemployed were whining wastrels, scum unemployable, treated as children on the one hand and dogs on the other. Today if you have votes—you are the bone and sinew of Englands greatness. 'You count.'

"It is a fact you may have forgotten. It is some time since you were so generally and emphatically reminded of it. It may be some time before you are so reminded of it again."

"But sufficient for the day, is the fact of your greatness— if you have votes. If you have not you are still clods cyphers, 'hands' merchandise. Get back to your hovels, your single room tenement, your sweat shops, back to your wage-slavery if you are fortunate enough to be employed, back to your whining wastrelism, to the outer darkness of impotent despair—if you are of the hungry multitude who lack the means of sustenance. Back, scum, to-day has nothing for you."

"But, if you have votes 'men of England, heirs of glory' you 'hardy sons of Labour,' then—England expects that every man this day will do his duty! And what is your duty?"

The leaflet went on to deal with the Political Parties, and their programme. This quotation is an example of the style of writing, and also a reminder of the fact that universal adult suffrage is quite recent.

In December 1906, Battersea Branch, proposed to contest the London County Council Elections. Comrades Fitzgerald, and Jackson, were chosen by the E.C. as candidates.. This action was challenged by the Edmonton Branch on the grounds that the policy of contesting these Elections was one for a Delegate Meeting to decide. The Delegates confirmed this form of activity at the January Meeting. It was later found that Jackson was not eligible as a candidate the final choice being J. Fitzgerald and M. Neuman. There is no evidence of these comrades having gone to the polls, so one presumes L.C.C. Elections have not been contested.

September of 1908 provided the next opportunity, with a Bye-Election at Haggerston, where a candidate named Burrows was standing for a reformist organisation. An article in the SOCIALIST STANDARD carried the title "The Harrying of Haggerston and the burying of Burrows." The article is too long to quote. It should be read as a fine example of political writing of the period. It had humour and sarcasm and is a joy to read, even to-day long after the event it is dealing with has been forgotten.

In 1908 it was the provincial Branch of Burnley having

a go. They sought, and obtained, permission for Comrade Tamlyn to contest the Gammon Ward, and Comrade Schofield the Whittleford Ward of Burnley. The total poll was 15 votes between them. The December SOCIALIST STANDARD said "We do not claim to have won either a numerical, or a moral victory, although our poll was minute we claim to have done some good, and are not dissatisfied with the results."

About the same time Tooting Branch put forward Comrades Cooper, Joy and Barker for the Tooting Ward, the result being 60, 58 and 56 respectively. The SOCIALIST STANDARD'S comment was: "We think we found fifty six supporters for the Revolution, and are encouraged in the hope that it is not altogether hopeless to appeal to the Electorate on the straight issue—Socialism."

1910 was a busy year for the Party in the Electoral field. In January 50,000 General Election manifestoes were printed and distributed. Space prohibits quotations from this leaflet so only a brief reference is possible. Like all leaflets of this type it deals with the political parties of the period, Tories, Liberals and Labour Party, and gave the Socialist Party attitude to the points raised.

Tottenham Branch was in the field of municipal Elections in April that year. With Comrade F. W. Stern for the High Cross Ward, and Comrade A. Anderson, F. G. Rourke in the St. Anns Ward, of the local Urban Council. The voting was Anderson 143, Rourke 67, F. W. Stern 63.

A Bye-Election at Walthamstow provided the local branch with the opportunity to issue a fine Eection leaflet.

In the same year there was a meeting of London members at Battersea, to discuss the action of Party members, if elected to local bodies. There does not appear to be any record of results of the discussion.

The Oath of Allegiance.

At the Annual Conference of 1910 electoral matters had a long discussion on a resolution from Manchester branch, "That any member elected to Parliament shall not take the oath of allegiance." That this resolution was tabled in spite of a decision by the 1909 Conference, "That the position of the Socialist Party of Great Britain, in reference to the oath of allegiance to Parliament, is that oaths and forms imposed by the constitution shall not be allowed to prevent elected representatives from taking their seats," showed the interest aroused by the issue. A resolution to send the question to branches was lost by 14 to 13 votes. Conference finally endorsed the 1909 ruling, and this was endorsed by a poll of the party and still stands as the Party position to-day. Since that year there have been no candidates put forward at municipal Elections.

Leaflets were, however, issued for the municipal elections of 1913, by the Watford Branch.

During the war years 1914-18 the party had a hard struggle to survive and there were no electoral activities. For the general election in December 1918 the front page of the SOCIALIST STANDARD, reproduced at the beginning of this article, showed the position of the Party.

The Move to Contest Parliamentary Elections.

The next move in Electorial Activity came in 1928. At a meeting of Party members, held in Friars Hall on Saturday, Feb. 25th, with seventy-nine members present, a resolution was moved by Higgs and Cash: "That this meeting of Party members declares itself in favour of running Socialist candidates, at Parliamentary Elections at the first opportunity, and, therefore, endorses the action of the E.C. in inaugurating a fund for that purpose." It was carried 41—18.

From this meeting can be traced the later developments in Electoral activity.

At the next General Election, in 1929, the E.C. agreed that Comrade Barker, of Tooting Branch, should be the prospective candidate for North Battersea, in opposition to Tory, Liberal, Labour and Communist candidates. An attempt was made to get the necessary funds, but it was hopeless, as the Parliamentary fund at that period showed a balance of £21 1s. 2d.

Battersea Branch were able to get in a good meeting at the local Town Hall, by using Comrade Barker in what has become known as a challenge meeting, at which the Tory and Liberal candidates put in an appearance. There was an audience of about nine hundred. This was the first gesture on the Parliamentary field.

For the next ten years Electoral activity was confined to issuing an occasional leaflet.

Electoral Activity in 1937 was a decision to contest one of the East Ham constituencies. Much work was done by bands of comrades in door to door canvassing. Meetings were held and Committee rooms were obtained, but activity was brought to an end by the outbreak of war in 1939.

After the Second World War.

The small amount of active work the Party was able to indulge in during the war years was followed by the 1945 election when, in Paddington North, the Party for the first time contested a Parliamentary Election. Members gave of their best to make the campaign a success. The weather was good, making outdoor meetings possible, and members were able to use the long June and July evenings for literature distributing and canvassing. The highspot of the Election, for those of us engaged in it, was the hiring and filling from top to bottom, of the Metropolitan Music Hall; a thrill which the writer of these words will never forget, thousands of men and women to hear the Socialist case. Finally, on July 5th, 1945, for the first time in the history of the working class movement, a Socialist offered himself for Parliamentary election, when the name of our Comrade Clifford Groves appeared on a voting paper.

The remainder of the story of the Party's activity in this field, is recent; the contesting of each By-Election, as they occurred in Paddington North, and the contesting of two seats at the 1950 Election. Paddington North, with Comrade McClatchie as the candidate, and East Ham South, with Comrade H. Young. Finally the last By-Election of November, 1953, with Comrade Waters as the candidate.

In all Elections the Party has entered, the results, judged by votes, have been very small, but that, of course, is not the standard by which Socialists judge the value of these activities.

This review of Party activities in the electoral field started out on a personal note, appropriate to the fact that it has been written for the Jubilee issue of the SOCIALIST STANDARD. May I, as one, who has had the good fortune to work on every Parliamentary Committee since 1929, send greetings to all those comrades, who by their efforts have made possible the work that has been done in this field, and hope they found joy, as I have in working together for our cause, Socialism   R. AMBRIDGE.

GREETINGS

FROM THE

U.S.A.

Just as we are going to press we can record a visit by two comrades from the World Socialist Party of America, comrades Rab and Gloss. This visit has shown how closely associated in principles and policy our two parties are. They addressed a number of outdoor meetings in London and the Provinces and the policy they expressed was undistinquishable from that expressed by our own speakers.

This welcome illustration of the fundamental unity of our two parties, although thousands of miles away from each other, augurs well for the progress of the Socialist movement. They take back with them memories of the warmth of their reception, and we hope it is the beginning of an international exchange of delegates.

It is fitting that this should have happened when we are celebrating our fiftieth anniversary.

We hope the day is not far distant when we can also welcome delegates from the Socialist Party of Canada and the Socialist Party of Australia and of New Zealand.

ADDRESSES OF COMPANION PARTIES

SOCIALIST PARTY OF AUSTRALIA, P.O. Box 1440M, Melbourne, Australia.

SOCIALIST PARTY OF CANADA, P.O. Box 115, Winnipeg, Manitoba, Canada.

SOCIALIST PARTY OF IRELAND, Sec. 32, Hanbury Lane, Meath St., Dublin, Eire.

SOCIALIST PARTY OF NEW ZEALAND, P.O. Box 62, Petone, New Zealand.

WORLD SOCIALIST PARTY OF THE UNITED STATES, Room 307, 3000 Grand River, Detroit 1, Michigan, U.S.A.

The SOCIALIST STANDARD, WESTERN SOCIALIST and other Socialist literature can be obtained from the above.

Correspondence for the Executive Committee and articles for THE SOCIALIST STANDARD *should be sent to the S.P.G.B., 52, Clapham High Street, S.W.4, London; 'phone: MAC 3811. Office hours: Monday, Wednesday, Thursday and Friday, 2 p.m. to 6 p.m.; Tuesday, 2 p.m.. to 9 p.m. Orders for literature to the Literature Secretary. Letters containing postal orders, etc., should be sent to E. LAKE, S.P.G.B., at the above address. P.O.'s, cheques, etc., should be crossed and made payable to the S.P.G.B.*

The Executive Committee meets every Tuesday at 52, Clapham High Street, S.W.4 (Head Office), at 7.30 p.m

RETROSPECT

The first number of the SOCIALIST STANDARD came out in September, 1904, a few years after the Boer War had ended and before World Wars had come into the picture. At that time the German Social Democratic Party had the support of millions, the Socialist Party of America was strong enough to put forward a candidate for the Presidency, in France, Austria and Italy, there were strong parties claiming to be Socialist, and even in the East the movement had spread—Russia, China and Japan, had small parties. Labour Parties and Welfare States had not yet emerged from the reformist womb, and the emptiness of nationalisation as a panacea for social ills had yet to be demonstrated.

To the uncritical it looked as if Socialism was " just round the corner." What they overlooked was the weakness of the parties that claimed to be Marxian and the futility of those that did not. All of them were tied to reform programmes that ultimately put out the fire of revolution they had lighted; all of them were dominated by the fatal principle of leadership and all of them collapsed under the blow of the first Great War.

On the first page of the first number of the SOCIALIST STANDARD there was an article from which we take the following paragraphs:—

" In the Socialist Party of Great Britain we are all members of the working class, and cannot hope that our articles will always be finely phrased, but we shall at least endeavour to lay before you on every occasion a sane and sound pronouncement on all matters affecting the welfare of the working class. What we lack in refinement of style we shall make good by the depth of our sincerity and by the truth of our principles."

. . . .

" In dealing with all questions affecting the welfare of the working-class our standpoint will be frankly revolutionary. We shall show that the misery, the poverty, and the degradation caused by capitalism, grows far more rapidly than does the enacting of palliative legislation for its removal. The adequate alleviation of these ills can be brought about only by a political party having Socialism for its object. So long as the powers of administration are controlled by the capitalist class so long can that class render nugatory any legislation they consider to unduly favour the workers."

That has been the outlook of the SOCIALIST STANDARD during the past fifty years.

The leading article of the first number set down in detail the position of the workers under Capitalism and the only solution to their problems. On another page our Declaration of Principles was printed, and it is exactly the same as has appeared in every issue since.

Everything of fundamental importance that had a bearing on Socialist policy has been thoroughly examined and discussed in the SOCIALIST STANDARD over the years.

The position and function of Trade Unions and the Socialist attitude towards them was the subject of discussion that appeared during some months of 1906. Industrial Unionism was the subject of numerous articles and correspondence from 1904 almost to the present day.

When the first Great War broke out in 1914 we printed our War Manifesto, in September of that year, in which we proclaimed our opposition to war, set forth the causes of war in the modern world, and pointed out that victory or defeat left the position of the workers, as a subject class, untouched.

When the Russian Revolution occurred in 1917 we printed an article which examined what lay behind that upheaval and stated, what subsequent history made plain, that it was not, and could not be, a Socialist Revolution. As information came along later we demonstrated from the facts available the accuracy of our original statement.

In 1926 we showed the weakness of the General Strike

and urged that, if the workers came out on strike they should do so in a body; if not successful within a short time they should go back in a body and not drift back. We pointed out that if they drifted back they would undo the work of years. In fact they were let down by the leaders they trusted and the masters were enabled to get rid of many limitations on their profit hunting that the workers had previously achieved.

In 1939, when the second Great War broke out, we reiterated the position we had put forward in 1914. In both wars our propaganda efforts suffered heavily. In the first war our speakers were arrested and our Head Office raided. In the second war we fared a little better but our Head Office suffered from bombing and it and much of our literature and records were destroyed.

In recent years we have put forward candidates for Parliament and our election literature has been reprinted in the SOCIALIST STANDARD.

In the course of fifty years the SOCIALIST STANDARD contains a faithful record of our work and our progress. In its columns will be found a mass of searching theoretical and historical articles that cover the main facts, principles, and policies, that are useful to the workers in their struggle to emancipate themselves from their subject position and to achieve the aim that we have unflaggingly put before them, the establishment of Socialism—a new form of society in which each will give according to his capacities and take according to his needs.

When the workers understand, accept and act upon the views we have been pressing to their notice the social ills they suffer from today will vanish like a bad dream.

THE STERILITY OF LABOURISM

To look for any underlying theoretical unity in the Labour Party is like looking for the proverbial black cat in a dark room—that isn't there. From scratch the organisation was opportunistic and eclectic. " We are committed to no one creed or dogma " was one of its earliest dogmas, while its adamant refusal to commit itself to any definite principle was the nearest approximation to a principle.

It was John Ward who said at a Labour conference prior to the Labour Party being formed " they wanted to get their feet planted in the House of Commons and should not be a bit particular the way they did it." While Keir Hardie and others present ostensibly protested at this, nevertheless the election pacts and arrangements between the Labour Party and Liberals, on whose support they relied, showed it was Ward's view which prevailed.

Because the political accommodation of the Labour Movement was broad it was able to house diverse and divergent ideas. Little wonder it spoke with many tongues. There were those preaching violent revolution. Others were the most gentle of evolutionaries regarding even the concept of class struggle as " bestial Darwinism," smuggled into " Socialist politics." Many were internationalists whose slogan was, " Workers of the World, Unite." Some were "Little Englanders " advocating " Britain for the British." There were militant atheists denouncing religion as the real enemy of Socialism, and devout Christians seeing " The New Testament " as the revealed and authorised Socialist catechism and Jesus the Socialist prototype.

Then there were the Fabians who subscribed, one might almost say, oversubscribed, to Harcourt's dictum, " We are all Socialists now." It was the Fabians who made State activity and Socialism, synonymous terms. In the howling desert of capitalism they discovered "Socialist" oases in the form of parks, playing fields, cemeteries, municipal baths, washhouses, and public conveniences, etc. Even the War Office and Scotland Yard had the character of Socialist institutions. Just as Liberal and Tory Governments might regard themselves as anti-Socialist but in so far as they carried on extensive and ever extending State activities were willy nilly instruments for Socialism. The Fabian policy of permeation or " boring from within," of various political parties was the political tactic to influence, " building up Socialism in one country."

Because the Fabians believed in "the silent revolution going on every day in our midst," some regarded the arrival of the Socialist party, i.e., the Labour Party, a little doubtfully. They thought that if this new party shouted Socialism at the top of its voice its revolutionary overtones might not only penetrate the ears of Liberals and Tories but into the fashionable drawing rooms of distinguished members of the Fabian Society with disturbing effects. To some Fabians it seemed that the thing most likely to retard Socialism, was Socialists. It was this "creeping Socialism" which, from the early battles of ideas, finally emerged victorious. It became the " official Socialism " of the Labour Party.

This Socialism is not a definite conception capable of actual realisation but an ideal to which there is only an imperceptable approximation. On the road to " Socialism " we shall meet many milestones which will tell us how far we have come. We shall not, however, meet any milestone which informs us how far we have to go before the Socialist goal is reached. Like the pilgrims on The Golden Road to Samarkand " . . . we shall go always a little further."

Nevertheless many pioneers of the Labour movement did not view Socialism as a merely recurring decimal of State activity. Many might have mistakenly believed that Nationalisation and various forms of State activity might serve as a means to an end but they did not believe that these things were an end in itself. Thus, Keir Hardie in accepting as he said " State Socialism," despite all its drawbacks, as an evolutionary stage in social development nevertheless held that it was " a preparation for free Communism in which the rule of life would be, from each according to his capacity to each according to his needs." (*From Serfdom to Socialism*, p. 89).

In fact a cursory glance at Labour literature prior to 1914 reveals sharp differences in outlook between present day Labourites and those of the past. At least many of the earlier ones had a sounder grasp of the essentials of capitalism and saw the alternative to present society as a social whole and not like the present ones as a thing of shreds and patches. One feels that many of the old stalwarts would have been astonished to learn that the Socialist objective is a mixed economy with its " Socialist " sectors and " private enterprise " sectors. Or that the theoretical basis of the new society is that piece of plagiarised Rousseauism, " The Managerial Revolution," preened of its sinister implications in order to fit in to current political requirements.

We may even note the exuberant vitality of the Fabian Fathers as compared with the indecisive and faded outlook of the Fabians unto the second and third generation. In the first Fabian Essays, perhaps the most radical of Fabian writing, the authors not only had very definite ideas about capitalism but a sublime faith in the way they were going to alter it. In the *New Fabian Essays* (1952) its authors are not only uncertain as to what capitalism actually is but even more uncertain what it is going to turn out to be. According to one of its authors, Mr. R. H. S. Crossman, the Labour Party has lost its way and it seems is not certain of finding it again. Thus the " official and authorised Fabian guide to British capitalism " turns out to be an uncharted voyage of discovery. Having no real knowledge of social navigation the New Fabians are fortified with the belief that this strange and experimental journey will if they go on and on finally get them somewhere—it will, but where?

It is not suggested that some basic change has taken place in the Labour Movement's outlook. In fact old views with new views have been so curiously mixed that it is impossible to separate one from t'other. The significant differences are to be found in the change of mood and sentiment. In the past many in the Labour Movement had at least a vision of an international organised working class transcending national barriers. They believed this was bound up with the growth of the movement. The advent of a Labour Party to power has had a totally opposite effect. The Labour Governments were inevitably emeshed in power politics with its concomitant power group notions and its idealogical division of good countries and bad countries. In such circumstances it not

only had to nullify the old international views but use its political and industrial influence among workers to actively suppress it. In far off days the Labour Party claimed that its accession to political strength would raise the standard of internationalism to a higher level. Today it lies in the political gutter.

In the past there existed in the Labour Movement a genuine militant sentiment. For many Pacifism was an article of " Labour " faith. By a supreme irony it was " Labour " as the governmental power who not only initiated peace time conscription but the greatest of all peace time rearmament drives. One can be a Pacifist Labour M.P. today advocating total disarmament but it is almost ·as anachronistic as an atheistic Republican on the Conservative front bench.

Undoubtedly the dynamic of the early Labour Movement was its political faith and vitality. A faith and vitality which succeeded in weaning the political allegiance of millions of workers from the old and powerful political parties of capitalism. Its weakness was rooted in its dualistic attitude. On the one hand it strove to be different from the older parties by its emphasis on social aims whose goal was the suppression of the existing order. On the other it might, and did, become a mass party dedicated to social reforms and was thus irrevocably committed to the assumption that capitalism was capable of indefinite and progressive improvement. From this it followed that their criticism of society took on an ethical rather than economic evaluation. If capitalism was capable of indefinite improvement then the failure of the old parties to have made any worthwhile progress lie in the fact it was administered " by hard faced politicians."—bad men—whereas it would be administed by good men—the Labour Party. Although if the pioneers were able to view present day capitalism they might, in spite of two Labour Governments, still think it was being run by bad men.

In short the Labour Movement failed to see the real nature of the social problem. They failed to see that British capitalism was an interlocked world system with no independent momentum of its own, or that the only way for a profit making system to act consistently is to make profit. In short they saw capitalism from the parochialism of a closed economy without seriously taking into account the internal distortions set up by external stresses and strains. Thus by abstracting from capitalism the concrete features which make it capitalism they proposed to administrate a capitalism which wasn't capitalism.

Moreover, the Labour Party in seeking mass support had to attract people who did not want capitalism changed but merely changes in capitalism. From that moment their ideals were not merely hampered but hamstrung. The need for popular support came into conflict with their avowed aims. The Labour Party by thus accepting this society was forced to work for it, not against it. So it repeats the age long story of social reformism the bartering of its beliefs and ideals for votes. It begins by declaring it will not play the game of capitalist politics. It ends by coming to power and accepting all the rules of the game and its youthful dreams become " the insubstantial pageant faded." If in this crazy world, haunted by uncertainty and fear and a neurotic impulse to self destruction, the Labour Party still has its dreams, then they are of the order of nightmares.

E. W.

A. ANDERSON

J. FITZGERALD

TWO OLD MEMBERS

Anderson and Fitzgerald were two of the most active members of the Party during the first 25 years of its existence. Anderson was a house-painter and Fitzgerald a bricklayer; and in the early days both of them were often out of work. Both were excellent indoor and outdoor speakers and debaters, both were members of the Executive Committee during the whole of that time, and both held their convictions strongly and argued them fiercely and forcefully. They were both very active in internal party controversies, though sometimes on the opposite sides.

Yet in spite of their similarities they were, in many respects, opposites.

Anderson was tall, rawboned, commanding; he was a first-class orator, with a high carrying voice, and could carry on speaking untiringly for hours at a stretch. He was at his best on the outdoor platform where his clarity, quick wits, rhetoric and caustic humour either drove his opponents into fits of laughter or reduced them to despair and impotent anger.

Fitzgerald, on the other hand. was short, compact, tough and had a deep powerful voice. He was at his best indoors. He prepared his material carefully, used simple language and put forward powerful logical and direct arguments, rarely employing humour or invective and never using rhetorical flourishes of any kind.

Anderson's chief activity was speaking and he organised the Party's outdoor propaganda in London for most of the time. He was in his element at rowdy spots where his forceful manner dominated the audience and quietened the disturbers. Before the Party was formed he was on the Provincial Executive of the Social Democratic Party and was active in Scotland.

Just before the 1914-18 war broke out the Party raised a fund to put a paid organiser into the field and Anderson was appointed to the job. The outbreak of war, and the difficulties into which the Party landed on account of it, put an end to the project.

In 1925 Anderson developed Arterio-sclerosis and died in 1926 at the early age of 47.

Although a regular and active speaker Fitzgerald's principal interests were writing and taking classes in economics. He was on the Editorial Committee of the SOCIALIST STANDARD from the early days until his death, and he wrote many excellent theoretical articles. He wrote the first article on the Russian Revolution, which appeared in the August, 1917, number and placed that upheaval in its proper perspective.

Fitzgerald was a first-class debater; two of the debates he represented the Party in were reprinted as pamphlets under the titles the " Conservative Party " and the " Liberal Party "—others appeared in the SOCIALIST STANDARD. The two that appeared in pamphlet form were reported verbatim and reading them discloses how clearly, simply and accurately, he spoke.

Fitzgerald was exceedingly helpful to young members. always willing and anxious to assist them in their studies by the loan of books, advice in their reading, and the resolving of knotty points.

In spite of his work for the Party Fitzgerald found

time for other studies. He passed an examination for building construction and, after a period, teaching mathematics to aspirants for the Indian Civil Service, he got a permanent job teaching at the Brixton School of Building.

Fitzgerald was an assiduous cyclist; he and the small-framed bicycles he designed for himself, were inseparable. He went to meetings and everywhere else on his bicycle, wet or fine.

In 1925 Fitzgerald contracted kidney trouble. He got temporary relief from an operation but the trouble returned again towards the end of 1928. He returned from a cycling holiday in Austria, Italy and Switzerland, to undergo two operations, and died in the spring of 1929 at the age of 56, a fortnight after the second operation.

Anderson and Fitzgerald, each in their own way, were sound guiding influences in the formative period of the Party's history. When they died in the twenties they were sad losses to the Party. They did their work during the toughest part of the Party's life when speaking was difficult, audiences hard to get, and the Party known to few, and they did not live to see the fruit of their labours.

GILMAC

PARTY PUBLICATIONS

The following is a list of pamphlets published by the Party during the past fifty years, with date of publication.

Party Manifesto	1905
Handicraft to Capitalism by Kautzky	1906
Art, Labour and Socialism by Wm. Morris	1907
The Working Class by Kautzky	1908
The Capitalist Class by Kautzky	1908
Socialism and Religion	1910
Socialist Party and The Liberal Party	1911
Socialist Party and Tariff Reform	1912
Socialism	1920
Why Capitalism will not Collapse	1932
Socialist Party and Questions of the Day	1932
Principles and Policy	1932
War and the Working Class	1936
Czech Crisis and the Workers	1938
Socialist Party Exposes Mr. Chamberlain	1938
Debate with Barbara Wootton	1940
Nationalization or Socialism	1945
Is Labour Government the Way to Socialism ?	1946
The Beveridge Plan	1946
Children's Allowances	1946
The Racial Problem	1947
Communist Manifesto and Last 100 Years	1948
Russia Since 1917	1948
Socialist Party and War	1950
Questions of the Day	New Edition

Revised editions of some of these pamphlets and numerous leaflets have also been issued.

A. E. JACOMB

A. E. Jacomb was an active member of the Social Democratic Federation at the end of the last century and the beginning of this, and was a member of a group which came out of that organisation to form the Socialist Party of Great Britain in 1904, helping to shape the Party's fundamental principles and policy. He was a compositor by trade and in the early years of the Party, in fact up to the beginning of the 'twenties, he was responsible for the printing of the SOCIALIST STANDARD and pamphlets. In this work he was a tower of strength, for the job was certainly not a sinecure. Often enough there were not sufficient articles to fill the paper and Jacomb had to make up the rest, under various pseudonyms, as he was doing the composing.

For many years, up to the end of the first Great War, Jacomb was a member of the Executive Committee and the Editorial Committee. He was a fine writer with a keen and caustic humour, contributing many excellent articles to the SOCIALIST STANDARD. He also drafted two of the Party pamphlets: " Socialism " and " The Socialist Party: Its Principles and Policy." He gave the best he could do to the Party although his life was one long struggle against financial difficulties.

It was a pitiful business that, towards the end of his life, Jacomb found himself in opposition to the Party about his attitude to the Spanish upheaval and to the last Great War, which led him to make a number of extravagant statements in the heat of controversy. But although he believed the policy of the Party was wrong, he still held fast to his fundamental socialist convictions. The vehemence of his criticism was due to his belief that the Party was on a wrong and fatal track, and to his anxiety to put it back again on what he thought was the right track.

Jacomb was a very fine character; simple and sincere, and a genuine and earnest champion of socialist principles for the whole of his long life.

He suffered from heart trouble for many years before his death in the autumn of 1946.

THE SOCIALIST STANDARD IN WAR TIME

From September, 1904, until the late twenties the SOCIALIST STANDARD was received from the printer in large flat sheets and had to be folded at Head Office. As soon as word was received that the paper would be delivered, generally on the last Saturday in the month members would gather round a table at Head Office and spend most of the afternoon and evening folding. During the folding discussions would be carried on about economics, history, or some of the many subjects that were in the air at the time. Members from the London branches would collect the branch quota and the parcels would be made up for posting.

During the 1914-18 war these jobs had to be carried on just the same. By 1916 the number of members who were able to carry on the Party work had been greatly reduced and those who were left were faced with many difficulties. Filling the columns of the *S.S.* became a major problem. Most of the regular writers were too busy keeping out of the Services to do much; one or two of them were able to send occasional articles from distant places. Consequently the supply of articles was scarce. There were also occasional difficulties with the printer who was dubious about printing some articles which, owing to their anti-war attitude, he feared would land him into trouble, though A. E. Jacomb, who did the compositing, was not the least bit disturbed. One article the printer refused at the last minute to print, and, as it was too late to replace, the *S.S.* was printed with a blank column. The blank column appeared in the *S.S.* for February, 1916, and was headed " Lloyd George and the Clyde Workers." In the middle of the column appeared the words:

" The firm who machines this paper has refused to print the article which was set up to appear under the above heading. We are therefore compelled to withdraw the article. We congratulate the Government on the success of their efforts to preserve the ' Freedom of the Press.' "

It is only fair to the printer to say that anyone who read that article now would have some sympathy for him: it was certainly pretty strong!

For the first eight months of the war the front page of the *S.S.* carried an article in large type dealing with the war; all except one were signed by the Executive Committee. The following were the titles, which are self-explanatory:—

September 1914. The War and the Socialist Position.
October. 1914. The Greater War, Our Appeal for Recruits.
November. 1914. Peace in the Hands of the Workers.
December 1914. The Real Foe.
January 1915. Under Martial Law.
February 1915. Socialism and the European " Socialists."

March 1915. A Russian Challenge. (This was a declaration by the Central Committee of the Russian Social Democratic Labour Party, signed by M. Maximovich, which the allegedly Socialist journals had refused to print.)
April 1915. Our Party Conference and the War. (This was another war manifesto.)

The July 1917 SOCIALIST STANDARD contained " The Manifesto of the Socialist Party of Great Britain to the proposed International Congress." This was a Congress of alleged Socialist Parties, relics of the Second International, whose proclaimed aim was to work out a policy for bringing about peace.

The Manifesto pointed out in detail how those invited to the Congress would go there with lies on their lips: they were neither Socialists nor anti-war, for they had already supported the war on one side or the other. This Manifesto reprinted two statements from our September 1914 Manifesto setting forth our attitude to the war and pointed out:—

" No matter which group of the Masters win the struggle, the Workers remain enslaved. The division of interest is not between the people of the world, but between the Classes— The Master Class and the Working Class. Not, therefore, in their fellow workers abroad, but in the Master Class at home and abroad, are the working-class enemies found.

" What interest have the Workers, then, in either starting or carrying on war for their masters? Absolutely none."

In July, 1918, the *S.S.* had to be cut down from eight pages to four owing to paper shortage. This was equivalent to eight pages of the present *S.S.*, because the size of leaf then was double the present size.

In August, 1918, the front page contained an article entitled " The Revolution in Russia; Where it Fails." This article summed up the position as far as the scanty information at the time would permit. The writer asks the question are the Russian people ready for Socialism and answers as follows:—

" Unless a mental revolution such as the world has never seen before has taken place or an economic change has occurred immensely more rapidly than history has ever recorded, the answer is ' No!' "

From the beginning to the end of the first Great War the SOCIALIST STANDARD maintained our Socialist attitude to war without qualification of any kind. Throughout the Second Great War it also held stedfastly to the same attitude."

GILMAC

UNDER MARTIAL LAW

" Those of our friends who lend support to our outdoor propaganda meetings will be aware that for the past week or two those meetings have been suspended. Also, readers of this issue will notice that the Lecture List which, until this date has appeared on the back page of this, our official organ, has now been withdrawn. These occurrences demand some few words of explanation, which are offered here.

" When the war broke out in August the Socialist Party unfalteringly proclaimed the Socialist position in relation to it. From our platforms and, at the first opportunity, in the columns of our organ, we took up the clear and definite attitude dictated by Socialist principles and working-class politics. This attitude, it is quite needless to say, was neither popular nor free from peril. It drew down upon us on the one hand the hostility of the rampant jingo hooligans of the streets, and on the other hand the ' patriotic ' fury of certain parasites ' dressed in a little brief authority.'

" Our object was not to bid defiance to a world gone mad, but to place on record the fact that in this country the Socialist position was faithfully maintained by Socialists. With this object in view we placed our backs against the wall and fought. Our platforms were smashed up and our members injured by mobs egged on by bourgeois cowards who, as usual, had not the spunk to do their own fighting for themselves. Not this only: one of our speakers was arrested and imprisoned, while others were dragged before the magistrates and bound over to keep the peace? In some instances the proceedings were rounded off by the victims being discharged from their employment by their ' good, kind masters ' for daring to hold political opinions of their own.

" We fought this fight long enough to achieve our purpose. In the columns of the last four issues of the SOCIALIST STANDARD stand recorded our action in this crisis, showing to the working class of the world that the Socialist Party in this country, acting in accordance with its declared principles, kept its hands clean in this, the most momentous crisis of its history. That is an asset to carry forward to the time when the war is finished.

" But now we are faced with a new situation. On the 28th of November last were issued Orders in Council (Defence of the Realm [Consolidation] Regulations) which render the prosecution of our propaganda a work of extreme peril. The following extracts from the Regulations will serve to show the nature of the impediment we are up against.

" 27. No person shall by word or in writing or in any newspaper, periodical, book, circular, or other printed publication spread false reports or make false statements or reports or statements likely to cause disaffection to His Majesty or to interfere with the success of His Majesty's forces by land or sea or to prejudice His Majesty's relations with foreign powers, or to spread reports or make statements likely to prejudice the recruiting, training, discipline, or administration of any of His Majesty's forces, and if any person contravenes this provision he shall be guilty of an offence against these regulations."

" 57. A person found guilty of an offence against these regulations by a court martial shall be liable to be sentenced to penal servitude for life or any less punishment."

In face of these restrictions and penalties the Executive Committee of the Socialist Party decided to suspend propaganda meetings for the time being, and called a meeting of Party members, at which meeting their action was endorsed.

We are aware, of course, that we lost a unique opportunity of indulging in heroics. We shall be told, perhaps, that we ought to have gone on in defiance of the powers that be till we went down in a blaze of fireworks. Our view, however, was the sane one dictated by our avowed principles. We have always held that the supreme power is in the hands of those who control the political machine. The most we could hope for by going on was to prove that contention. But it is not for us to prove our contentions by acting in opposition to them.

" There was no question of fighting for Socialism or Socialist principles. The Regulations were not, as far as we could judge, in the nature of anti-Socialist legislation. They were merely the precautions ordinarily resorted to by countries embroiled in a serious war. For this very reason we had nothing to gain by running counter to the Regulations, for just as the temper of the working class is, at the moment, such as to prevent them benefiting from our propaganda, so it would prevent them learning anything from our victimisation or martyrdom. Clearly, then, it was our tactics to place ourselves in such a position that only by the Regulations being strained to the point where they would become obviously anti-Socialist could we fall victims to them. These tactics demanded, in view of the risk of having our spoken words twisted and distorted in the courts, that we suspend propaganda meetings for the time, and confine our activities to such forms of propaganda as would secure us from any attack that did not reveal the deliberate intention of our opponents to crush us under the cloak of the present situation."

(The above article appeared on the front page of the SOCIALIST STANDARD for January 1915.)

CHARLES LESTOR

I first met Charlie Lestor over 30 years ago. I was still a kid, he was a mature and impressive man. His effect on the eager audiences of the post 1914-18 war was electric.

He had just arrived in this country after 20 years in Canada and the U.S.A. His Canadian style, accent and rig made him remarkable enough; his address to the large audiences of unemployed ex-servicemen was extraordinary. When most of the I.L.P. and Communist "Unemployed organisers" devoted their attention to personal invective against individual ministers; or the usual temporary nostrums for increase of the dole, or (much more) prevention of its decrease. Lestor never failed, in my hearing, at least, to go straight to the root of the matter.

He just could not speak to an audience without dealing with the capitalist system. From that day to this, I have never wavered in the opinion that of all the speakers I have heard, Lestor, in those days, was out on his own as a powerful exponent of Marxian economics in a popular trenchant style.

In clipped and rugged American terms, without a word wasted, he would grip a large audience from the first phrase and proceed to build up a rigorously logical exposition of surplus value.

"There's no sentiment in Business," "that profit is wrung out of the hides and carcases of the working-class," "those wages amount to just enough fried fish, chips and beer to keep you working."

These and similar phrases were as typical of Charlie Lestor as the shock of hair, the bushy eyebrows covering the twinkling eyes, and the missing index finger on the waving hand. Tanned by the prairie suns and the Yukon snows as at home in 'Frisco or Winnipeg as in Stepney or Hyde Park, he was a modern cosmopolite, a man of all countries and all trades.

For many years I lost touch, but immediately remade his acquaintance on joining the S.P.G.B. in 1939. Much water had flown under the Bridge, the years were beginning to take their toll. In the bitter weather of 1941 it was Charles Lestor who attended regularly at the Gloucester Place office of the Party, in a Balaclava hat, sometimes with frost on his eyebrows, to give instruction and counsel to young members in between air raid warnings. Subsequently I read through the minutes of those talks which covered a wide field of History, Economics and Current Affairs.

In 1945, the post of full-time propagandist fell vacant. At an age when most men ask nothing more than their carpet-slippers Lestor applied and was appointed. As Central Organiser of the Party at the time, I went over to see him in N.E. London, and made sure, as it was snowing heavily, that he had some reasonably warm equipment for the bitter trip to Glasgow that night.

The years passed rapidly by, and many were the demands of the Party on Lestor's services. I cannot recall one occasion when these were refused or denied. Whether the meeting was large or small, far or near, early or late, he accepted as a matter of course.

As time marched on, it became apparent that even a man as vigorous, tough and energetic as Charlie Lestor could not beat Anno Domini indefinitely. Still the indomitable spirit refused to give up. In weather when he should have been indoors at home, he was regularly at Lincolns Inn and Tower Hill. The once powerful and strident tones which would ring out like a blast across a large audience, were sinking into an almost inaudible whisper.

Never did his sense of humour desert him, his remarks were now often punctuated by a quiet chuckle. He tended, in later years, to an exaggerated optimism with regard to Socialism which other well-known Socialist speakers have also expressed.

During the Party's tenure of Rugby Chambers he once remarked to me "When you've stopped learning, you've stopped living." Surely that explains the astounding tenacity with which he stuck to his efforts as a Socialist propagandist, for so long.

HORATIO.

SOME THEORETICAL QUESTIONS

Through having a formal Declaration of Principles to act as basis for membership and for the control of conduct, and through the use of Marxian economics and explanation of social change, the S.P.G.B. has maintained a continuity of outlook unknown in organisations guided largely by the mood and circumstances of the moment. But continuity has not meant refusal to recognise changes of capitalist trends or the emergence of important new information.

Marxian economic conceptions, in spite of the continous stream of disparagement from critics, have shown themselves remarkably robust in serving to explain the workings of the capitalist system under modern developments. One illustration is the great rise of the price level in the last forty years. While reformist parties have offered " explanations " which consist of little more than attributing the rise of prices to the wickedness of capitalists and the cowardice of governments,, Marxism economics enables us to see that the overwhelmingly largest factor has been the devaluation of the currency in terms of gold, in U.S.A., to about one half and in Great Britain to about one-third of the value before World War I.

Examination of current economic problems from the Marxian standpoint enabled the S.P.G.B. to show the absurdity of the periodical waves of currency crankism such as the Douglas Scheme; the truth that rates and taxes, in spite of their deceptive appearance, are a burden on property not on the workers' wages and that war likewise is paid for by the capitalist class; and that while wages do not merely follow prices—other factors including the workers' struggles play a part—the belief that lower prices mean prosperity for the workers is a delusion.

In all these matters economic understanding reinforced the S.P.G.B.'s political principles and saved it from floundering in the confusion that fogged the reformists.

Special reference needs to be made to economic crises. Marx's valuable material on capitalism's economic crises was published after his death in Volumes II. and III. of *Capital* in virtually the incomplete form in which he left it—he had not reached the stage of rounding it off into a comprehensive whole. In the hands of later writers, friendly, critical, and hostile alike, who have overlooked this, Marx's tentative and piecemeal conclusions have sometimes proved to be dangerous half-knowledge, and many are the explanations of and prophecies about, crises that have not stood up to the test of events; including some by the S.P.G.B. But this has not been of too great importance because the S.P.G.B. was never dependent on crises and crises theories in the way the Communists and some other groups have been. The S.P.G.B. has never been in the position of some reformists of believing that capitalism is only open to condemnation during crises and not during its boom periods; or in the position cf Communists of believing that capitalism can only be got rid of through a crisis, a collapse.

This belief has a long history and it has been the S.P.G.B. alone which set itself firmly against it.

When Marx and Engels were first approaching the subject of crises they thought, on the evidence then available, that crises happened at shorter and shorter intervals, each one worse than the one before. They soon dropped the first and worked on the supposition that crises happen about every ten years; and they later recognised that it was possible for a relatively acute crisis to be followed by a mild one. It is, however, probable that Marx, and certain that Engels, thought that the general trend was for crises to become worse. This came out most markedly after Marx's death when we find Engels in 1884, under the influence of the prolonged " Great Depression," believing that the 10 year cycle had gone and that permanent depression had taken its place; and writing two years later that " we can almost calculate the moment when the unemployed . . . will take their fate into their own hands."

Just as 30 years earlier, in 1856, he had expected the coming economic crisis to end capitalism, so he now thought in 1886 that unemployment would drive the workers to revolt; and seven years later he was pinning his hopes on the crisis he anticipated from America's invasion of world markets.

Nobody could hold a theory that crises become worse and worse without being at least strongly tempted to believe that this could not go on indefinitely; a time must come when the crisis would be too great for recovery to be possible. This notion was gratefully taken up by many groups, including the Communists and the I.L.P., for they had dire need of some such theory. How else could they envisage the end of capitalism? The Communists never accepted the S.P.G.B. case that capitalism would be ended by the positive action of a majority understanding Socialism. Instead they trusted in leadership of the discontented masses by an intellectual minority and they welcomed the notion that an economic crisis would provide the opportunity.

The I.L.P. had earlier believed that the road to emancipation was through Labour Party pressure in Parliament for reforms, especially under Labour government. But by the 1931 crisis, after two Labour Governments, the I.L.P. leaders could no longer be enthusiastic for this and they gladly swallowed the " collapse " theory which promised an easy and early alternative.

The S.P.G.B., which had never needed such a theory, never entertained it and in 1932 marked its opposition to the then popular collapse doctrine by publishing a pamphlet "Why Capitalism will not Collapse," in which was reaffirmed the Party's view that " until a sufficient number of workers are prepared to organise politically for the conscious purpose of ending Capitalism, that system will stagger on indefinitely from one crisis to another."

Because the S.P.G.B. has this firmly based and comprehensive Socialist case against capitalism and is not dependant on particular temporary trends of capitalism, it could view with equanimity unforeseen new developments and reversals of trends that have seriously shaken other organisations. The S.P.G.B. never mixed up State capitalism with Socialism and was therefore able from the start to examine critically the organisation, and finances of nationalisation and expose both the Labour Party propaganda asking working class support for it and the equally fraudulent campaigns against it carried on by sections of the capitalists and by the Tory and Liberal parties. The limited progress made by nationalisation in the U.S.A. and many other countries (contrary to Engels' expectation 60 years ago), and the present perhaps temporary flow of the tide against nationalisation do not at all affect the S.P.G.B. case though they profoundly disturb the reformists to whom nationalisation meant something different and so much more important.

The S.P.G.B., while opposed to building up an organisation on a reform programme, never accepted the two ideas that from time to time have obtained wide acceptance in Labour circles, that the capitalists either would not concede reforms or that they could not afford to do so. So the rise first of unemployment insurance (not foreseen by Engels and others who foretold unemployed revolt) and later of more comprehensive schemes has not in any way affected the basic case of the S.P.G.B. against capitalism.

Nor has the S.P.G.B. case needed to be modified because of the growth in trade union membership and changes in structure and activities. Members of the S.P.G.B. could be and were keenly interested in discussing trade union trends, forms of organisation, strike tactics, etc., but all of these aspects were secondary ones viewed in the light of the recognition that trade union action cannot end capitalism and establish Socialism. The " general strike " of 1926 was for the S.P.G.B. a complete confirmation of views long before thought out and discussed by members. The " general strike," that is to say united action to hold up industry as a whole, had been advocated in the SOCIALIST STANDARD four years before (Feb. 1922) as the only means of meeting the general attack on wages. The three guiding conditions then insisted upon were that the stoppage should not be prolonged, it would succeed in its object quickly or not at all; that it should be carried out peacefully for its limited objective with no encouragement of riot or destruction to give excuse for the use of the armed forces; and that the decisions to come out and go back should be in the hands of the rank and file and not entrusted to leaders. In the event it was misguided trust in leadership that made the strike of 1926 less impressive and effective than it could

have been, though the S.P.G.B. certainly had never encouraged illusions as to what could be hoped for from such a strike.

On war there has been some development in the Party's attitude due to events stimulating deeper consideration. In 1904 it seemed sufficient to explain war between capitalist powers (and their wars of colonial expansion) and to insist that the workers had no interest in the issues behind war; rounding this off with denunciation of capitalist greed and capitalist cruelty. Little was said of the attitude of Marx half a century earlier of being prepared to support one side in war either on the ground that the outcome would be an advantage for the democratic and working class movements (e.g. the defeat of reactionary Russia), or that the workers should resist aggression against the country they live in. Had this question been raised as a live issue in 1904 there can be no doubt that the Party would have decided then (as it did nearly 30 years later) that Marx was mistaken in thinking that results worth while for the working class or for the speeding up of the introduction of Socialism could result from waging war. That the S.P.G.B. should have reached a conclusion different from his was due partly to the fact that, looking back, we could see that his hoped for beneficial results did not happen; partly to realisation of the tremendous barrier to Socialism presented by nationalism; partly to the much greater magnitude and destructiveness of the weapons and organisations of war; but basically to the S.P.G.B.'s unique appreciation of the importance of understanding in the achievement of Socialism. For us it was unthinkable that lack of understanding could be compensated for by use of force. Hence the affirmation in a lengthy statement on war formally adopted by the Party that " war is not an instrument that can be used by Socialists or supported by Socialists."

The Party's original condemnation of unscientific emotionalism and insistence on the need to understand the causes and methods of social and ideological change and of the emergence of new forms has stood every test. The early issues of the SOCIALIST STANDARD contained many articles and answers to correspondents on this issue and the article " Unscientific Emotionalism " in the issue for December, 1914, will show how adequately the problems were understood by that time. The following are extracts: —

" When our method of reasoning is applied back through history, we find that man's thoughts have always been governed by his inherited notions and the material conditions surrounding him; and as these conditions have centred round the obtaining of food, clothing and shelter, so at each period of social history the more or less clear relations that were built up on this basis (the particular relations that existed at the particular time between the various producers and distributors of the social wealth) have been reflected in the mind in a correspondingly more or less clear manner. After the break up of the early tribal communities society was split into various classes, and history since then has been the record of the struggles of each class in its turn to control society for its own advantage. When the progress of the method of producing wealth had reached a certain point the class in society that was taking the principal part in production found the old laws (that were suitable to the old governing class) placed a restriction on their further development. The problem of the removal of all these restrictions therefore constantly occupied them, and it is then forced home to their minds that the only solution to the problem of the removal of these restrictions is the control of society by themselves, and the alteration of the existing laws to suit the new conditions. Just so at present the spectacle of the workers doing all the work of the world forces home to the minds of men the socialist view that if the workers produce and distribute all the wealth of society they therefore should own it, and reap the benefit of their work themselves, instead of supporting a group of idlers and good-for-nothings. The solution of the problem is contained within the problem itself. ' Therefore mankind always takes up only such problems as it can solve' (Marx)."

The article showed how the ideas of equality that had lain dormant in the minds of men since the break up of tribal Communism, had been exploited in the past by particular propertied classes struggling for supremacy and wanting the support of the oppressed, and were being exploited now by reformist bodies that did not understand the nature of the problem. The following further extract is a fitting note on which to end this brief survey of some aspects of Socialist theories.

"The socialist reasons from the practical affairs of everyday life to general conclusions, while the emotionalists set out with a plan formed in accordance with certain abstract ideas true for all time (!) without taking account of the historical development of society. They try to organise society according to the idea instead of recognising that the shape their particular ideas take has been formed by society."

H.

SOCIALIST LITERATURE

★ **SOCIALISM**

A concise exposition of the subject in language which all can understand 48 pages: 4d.

★ **THE RACIAL PROBLEM**

A survey of the historical, political and economic causes of race prejudice, its dangers and its solution. 78 pages: 1s.

★ **RUSSIA SINCE 1917**

This reprint of articles from the " Socialist Standard " shows why the Russian upheaval could not be a socialist revolution; and shows the consistency of the Socialist Party's attitude towards Russia since 1917. 114 pages: 1s.

★ **THE SOCIALIST PARTY AND WAR**

Explodes various false theories about the cause of war and explains the nature of the capitalist rivalries leading to armed conflict. 100 pages: 1s.

★ **NATIONALISATION OR SOCIALISM ?**

An interesting examination of the history and meaning of nationalisation and its relation to Socialism. 68 pages: 6d.

★ **THE COMMUNIST MANIFESTO— AND THE LAST HUNDRED YEARS**

A reprint of the famous Manifesto together with our own historical account of the working class movement since 1848. 92 pages: 1s.

★ **" QUESTIONS OF THE DAY "**

An extensively revised edition of with several new chapters is now on sale. 123 pages: 1s.

All the above can be ordered from bookstalls, or can be sent direct, postage 2d. extra, from the Socialist Party of Great Britain, 52, Clapham High Street, London, S.W.4.

" CITIES AND THRONES AND POWERS "

It is difficult to parcel history. We place the feudal age between 500 and 1,500 A.D., and at once have to add there was chattel slavery after the beginning and capitalism before the end of it. When did modern European history begin? A dividing line has to be drawn, and sufficient reason found for it. Most historians agree on the French Revolution as the convenient starting point: there is an intelligible, unbroken series of events that began in 1789. The Socialist Party was founded ten years before it reached its climax.

The outbreak of war in 1914 is often represented as a surprise—England on its August holidays, douched by the unforeseen. In fact, everyone knew it was coming. The Dual and Triple Alliances of the eighteen-nineties defined the position with painful clarity: the great European nations ranged in two hostile groups, each piling armaments and watching for advantage. Popular papers in Britain carried pictures of German militarism—stiff-legged marching regiments, the Kaiser in his spiked helmet —while Haldane reorganized the British army on German lines and France, Austria, Russia and Italy trained their conscript armies. No country could afford to fall behind: " You cannot when other nations are spending huge sums of money which are not merely weapons of defence but are equally weapons of attack," said Lloyd George.

While the larger powers circled and feinted, the small ones were at one another's throats. Montenegro, Serbia, Novibazar, Albania—a dozen states in the Balkans with names that, twenty years later, ring of mustachios and musical comedy. Each of them was land-hungry and full of aggressive nationalism; all of them were caught in the struggle between Russia, Germany and Austria, for passage to the Mediterranean and the East.

Politically, it was a Machiavellian decade of plot and counter-plot—fundamentally, the seethings of a grand-scale eruption of imperialism and international competition. From 1870 onwards Germany had undergone a swift economic growth like that of Britain a hundred years before. Huge industrial combines emerged, trade multiplied, colonization started; shipping increased, and there was tariff protection against American and British goods. Britain had made its empire, held the markets and the sea routes; Germany was the rival, the strongest competitor. Many of the other European nations were still semi-feudal, but their growing commercialism (or that of their neighbours) drew them into the vortex.

The war changed the nature of European politics. Inevitably, it changed the map; its course included the Russian Revolution and the American entry to the arena.

World Politics, 1904-1954

The relics of feudalism were swept away. While Russian aristocrats scurried across Europe for asylum, the Austro-Hungarian empire which had dominated central Europe was reduced to a small republic. The technical needs of twentieth-century warfare gave tremendous impetus to industry everywhere. And, at the end of the war, America was creditor to all Europe on a near-fantastic scale. Production for profit there had to be.

The Peace Treaties were shrewdly savage arbiters of the new balance of power. The principle that the beaten country must pay had been imposed by Germany on France in 1871; now it was imposed on Germany by France and Britain. The attitudes of the victorious nations differed, however. Britain had " raked in "—German ships, spheres of influence in the Middle East, spoils for the Dominions—and needed now a prosperous, buying-and-selling Germany; France's desire was for Germany stripped and subjugated. America withdrew politically but remained economically, bestriding the narrow, exhausted European world like a colossus.

By 1922 it was evident that, whatever had been intended at Versailles, German economic recovery had to be not merely allowed but encouraged. It is worth saying at this point, that the Socialist Party was not mistaken in its commentary before, during or after the war. The four years' havoc was the inevitable climax to the commercial struggle which had spread and intensified for a hundred years. German militarism, which mostly took the blame, was simply the expression of a rapid, aggressive capitalist growth; given slight variations in nineteenth-century history, the enemy could as easily have been France or Russia. Many people in Britain were not patriots in the conventional sense but believed that to break German capitalism would bring jobs and prosperity. In the first wartime issue of the STANDARD facts and figures were quoted to prove them wrong, and wrong they were: mass unemployment began in 1920 and continued till 1939. The post-war world was shaped by capitalism, not by statesmen.

The steps to rehabilitate German economy were precipitated by the Germans' attempt to evade astronomical debts by devaluing the mark. In a few months half a million marks were worth only a penny, and when the Germans reformed their currency the franc fell in turn. America, France and Britain, with scarcely an altruistic motive between them, collaborated to make Germany solvent and revive its industry. Five years' flourishing trade and high profits followed. They ended as abruptly as they began when the 1929 crash caused the withdrawal of American money from Germany and the collapse that paved the way for Hitler.

Meanwhile the " new civilization " was transforming Russia, and its votaries formed the Third International. The war had killed the second; its members, the social-democrats and the labour leaders, supported the conflict they had pledged themselves to oppose. The doctrine of capitalism's impending collapse became a spearhead of " left-wing " political theory, seemingly given weight by the instability of finance, commerce and governments in Western Europe. The Russian Revolution's effect on post-war world politics was mainly indirect, inspiring new ideologies and policies; the looked-for European uprising never came, and it was twenty years before Russia figured largely on the scene.

The peace treaty had set up the League of Nations, a permanent, elaborately-organized machine for conciliation and arbitration between nations. America was not a member, nor was Germany until 1926. Its Court of International Justice at The Hague was to consider all quarrels between member-states; it sought reduction of armaments, above-board diplomacy, and co-operation between governments. There is a story that Abraham Lincoln, when his two little boys were in tears and a stranger asked the matter, answered: " Just what's the matter with the whole world—I've got three apples and each wants two." It was much the same for the League, except that " wanting two " was economic necessity and the other nations' reactions to disputes depended not on their ideals but on their interests. From 1925 onwards, every country was rearming. When the League disapproved, they left it.

The inter-war period has been called " the long week-end." By the mid-thirties, Monday morning's business was plain. After the depression, competition was fiercer than ever before. Cheap mass-produced goods from America and the East flooded across the tariff frontiers of Europe; the Lancashire mill girl stood in Japanese stockings and waved a Japanese Union Jack at the Coronation of George the Sixth. Italy, empire-hungry, flouted the League and attacked Abyssinia; Britain, with less fuss, annexed a hundred thousand square miles of Southern Arabia, breaking twenty-year-old pledges to the Arabs. Japan, too, lapsed from agreements with the western nations when driven by the same commercial interests to attack China. Pacts and treaties could mean little in the inescapable struggle for markets and empires.

The Spanish Civil War provided a bargaining counter for the European powers, and established anti-Nazism and anti-Fascism as positive political faiths for which the coming world war was to be fought. From early 1938, when Austria was seized, all eyes were on Nazi Germany. Needing still to expand, barred from movement to the west, the Germans went to Czechoslovakia, the most highly industrialized section of the old Austro-Hungarian empire. The hour seemed to have come. The British government, however, incompletely prepared for a European war and with little prospect of gain from it, delayed the outbreak.

Through 1939, frank preparations were made in every country. Japan, still attacking British interests in the East, was Germany's ally. The signal for war was the Russo-German pact in August, and the invasion of Poland its swift consequence. The prevention of another power's dominating Europe was traditional, necessary foreign policy for Britain; Germany, still aggressive with success, had spread across the centre and the east and was within sight of the Rumanian oilfields and the way to the Mediterranean.

Russian imperialism showed its hand long before Russia entered the war; the hand was taken by Britain and America at the Yalta Conference in 1945, when the division of the post-war world was privately arranged. Russia was granted territory and spheres of influence in the Orient, and took them in Eastern Europe. Both coming late into the fighting, America and Russia tower in the war and its aftermath. The doctrine of the balance of power gave way to clear recognition of two great hostile camps of nations across the world, with convalescing Japan the unknown quantity and United Nations continuing the League of Nations' losing struggle for world harmony.

The pattern of these fifty years, then, has been one of expansion; commercial expansion, and with it expansion in the conflicting political units. In 1904, Europe was the bone of contention for a crowd of scuffling puppy-nations. Today it is the world, contested by two great powers and their dependencies. The proposal of a federated Europe, first made in 1940, has been taken seriously since the war; national boundaries, so long considered an obstacle to Socialism, are being erased by capitalism.

Fifty years' international strife. The Socialist Party has commented on but never entered it; it has opposed all wars because the working class can gain nothing from them, has been pilloried for saying so, and lived to see that it was right and the others wrong. World politics are capitalist politics: bluffings, courtships, threatenings and ultimately killings for markets, materials and communications. Not many people care much for the rights of small nations, but everybody cares for his interests in small nations. Men of goodwill and ill will have wrestled to control the consequences of competition; the truth is that they will continue as long as capitalism continues.

R. COSTER.

FIFTY YEARS AGO

(From the Socialist Standard, September, 1904)

" How comes it that the men and women who till the soil, who dig the mine, who manipulate the machine, who build the factory and the home, and, in a word, who create the whole of the wealth, receive only sufficient to maintain themselves and their families on the border line of bare physical efficiency, while those who do not aid in production—the employing class—obtain more than is enough to supply their every necessity, comfort and luxury?

To find a solution to this problem is the task to which the Socialist applies himself. He sees clearly that only by studying the economics of wealth-production and distribution can he understand the anomalies of present-day society. He sees, further, that having gained a knowledge of the economic causes of social inequality, he must apply this knowledge through political action—through the building up of a Socialist organisation for the capture of Parliament and the conquest of the powers of government."

MOSES BARITZ

Moses Baritz was one of the most forceful and courageous characters who ever entered the ranks of the S.P.G.B. Of less than average height, bulkily built and with a stentorian voice, he was a ruthless and merciless man to meet in political debate. He had an uncanny memory, was a terror to his opponents and sometimes an embarrassment to his friends.

He was a Manchester man and much of his political work was done in his native city, and London. He was also active in the U.S.A. and Australia. In 1919 he was invited by comrades to give a series of lectures in New Zealand. On landing in that country he was met by detectives who shadowed him during his brief stay. He became a torment to New Zealand labour leaders and was soon arbitrarily deported. Finding it difficult to enter another country he spent some time on the sea to the annoyance of the shipping company.

Of the numberless anecdotes about Baritz's political activities we can give only one. Once, in Manchester, forcefully debarred from entering a meeting to be addressed by H. M. Hyndman of the old Social Democratic Party, because it was known that he would be an annoyance to the speaker, Baritz climbed on to the roof and blew his clarinet down the ventilator shaft until he was enticed down and allowed to take his seat in the hall.

Later in life his detailed knowledge of music secured him a responsible job with a well known gramophone and radio company where he was highly valued. He broadcast on musical subjects on several occasions, and frequently combined his musical knowledge with his Socialist propaganda. Failing eyesight caused him to wear pebble lens spectacles and in the 1930's his bulky frame, white curly hair and dominant voice, were met with mixed feelings by men of all political parties throughout this country. When he died in April, 1938, at the age of 54 the S.P.G.B. lost a treasured and colourful personality.

W. WATERS.

FROM AN OLD AUSTRIAN COMRADE

During my stay in England, some 40 years ago, I came in contact with your party whose teaching brought me out of the political quandary and wilderness in which I had till then been groping under the influence of Austrian Social Democracy. A study of economics and especially Karl Marx's critical scientific analysis of the operation of the profit-making system, to which study I had been encouraged, was a veritable revelation. What I had previously been taught in Continental labour, "socialist" and "communist" circles and in Arbeiter-Zeitungen, and what is still being propagated to this day as being Socialism or Communism, or "instalments of socialism," revealed itself as the very opposite, namely the consolidation and strengthening of capitalism. So far indeed from touching or interfering with the fundamental principle of private or State-capitalist ownership of the means and instruments of wealth-production and distribution so far from touching the degrading fundamental status of the workers as a disinherited slave-class to capital, the policy of all the so-called Socialist and Communist parties in the world—save the Socialist Party of Great Britain and its companion parties overseas based on their Declaration of Principles—merely serves to prevent the breakdown of, and so to perpetuate the rule of capital and money.

The 60 years of Austrian "socialism" or "instalments of socialism" have proved the truth of this contention. With "socialist" governments in a number of countries, with "socialist" State-presidents, Prime-ministers and Chancellors in others, with three times Labour party governments in Britain up to now, with "communism" in one sixth of the earth, capital and its privileged beneficiaries, the shareholders, the millionaires, Royal families, kings and queens, landlords and aristocrats, the high priests and dignitaries of the church, and the rest of the masters' supporters, are doing as well as ever. They can indeed feel quite safe in their palaces, castles and luxurious mansions, as long as the workers and their families do not ask the impertinent question where their "instalments of socialism" are, or as long as they believe their leaders' assurances that the working-class has been "uplifted" from wage-slavery to "free men." What a farce!

Already at an early stage of my contact with the English comrades and my discussions with them—what a different picture was unrolled before my mental eye! I came to realize that as the very antithesis of capitalism, the term Socialism can mean nothing but the total abolition of private and State-ownership of the means of life and their conversion into the SOCIAL or COMMON property of the people as a whole. It had never struck me

before that the true implications of such a new constitution of society and the completely changed outlook on every phase of human co-existence it is bound to produce, were never dwelled upon in so-called socialist publications. Ignoring, as they do, these implications, the leaders and mouthpieces of the big parties maskerading under the banner of Socialism, would seem to look upon a classless and moneyless society as a utopia, or else they are deliberate frauds. As a result of "socialist" education and propaganda provided by these workers' organisations, most of their members will indeed tell you that a society without wages and without money—a society based on the principle: "From each according to his capacity, to each according to his NEEDS" was an impossibility, a utopia. How pleased the capitalists must be with such loyalty of their slaves to capitalism! Well, dear brother, while wage-packets are a cardinal feature of their system of exploitation, they will have *no* place under socialism, since there will be no employers and no employed. There will only be co-operation in producing the wherewithall to live and enjoy life by so doing. The very word "work" will become generally identified with pleasure. Wealth will no longer be produced for buying and selling for profit, but for U S E. Commerce will be replaced by distribution according to the needs of individuals the world over. With no more buying and selling, and no more money (which becomes unnecessary with the abolition of private property and will go into the museums for future generations to see and marvel at 20th century-man's folly), there will of course also be no more buying and selling of human labour power (wages), no prostitution male or female, and no corruption. The dependence of individuals on other individuals or groups of individuals will cease. Since under socialism the means of subsistence, including all cultural needs and desires, will be guaranteed by society to every human being from the cradle to the grave, irrespective of services rendered, there will be no more need for insurance of any kind, nor pensions. The sick and infirm, the invalids and the old will naturally be provided for as well as the children.

With the gigantic means of production and distribution now at the disposal of mankind, all man's needs and desires can easily be satisfied, especially when the enormous waste due to the protection of the private property "rights" by armaments, police, laws, insurance, etc. ceases, and all the complicated and intricate machinery of financial accounting, Banks, advertising, taxes, and the rest of the capitalist paraphernalia is no longer necessary. As there will be no more private or State-ownership, there can be no more coercion. Government, which is only the executive committee for the management and safeguarding of the interests of property-holders and the maintenance of privilege, will be replaced by a purely technical administration of things. With private interests and the question " does it pay " out of the way, it will be a comparatively simple process. In fact. most of the complications and problems with which society has to grapple today, will fall away. With the world and all its resources controlled and operated by, and in the interest of the people as a whole, as their common heritage, with all separating frontiers gone, as they will under socialism, not only poverty, but insecurity and the rest of the social evils arising therefrom, will be things of the past.

Mankind under socialism will no longer be dependant, for the continuance of life, on the crops and dwellings in this or the other locality. If they are destroyed, no one who is not himself destroyed or struck down by the event, need suffer prolonged hardship; it will simply be a case of perhaps only temporary displacement until " his " devastated area has by common effort or desire been restored. Apart from this, mankind will not be slow in learning from the experience and probably take greater precautions against possible " accidents " and riotous nature in future. Anyway, the destruction and devastation wrought by natural catastrophies is as nothing compared with the havoc and ruin caused through capitalist wars and preparations for war, and the latter will certainly be things of the past under socialism.

Only the revolutionary objective of the S.P.G.B. is worthy of the name of Socialism; what goes today by that name. i.e. what is by present-day " socialist, communist " and labour parties represented and claimed to be Socialism, is a fraud, a delusion and a snare. To have allowed themselves to be misled and bamboozled by this lure, has not been without a heavy penalty for the workers and their families. By identifying themselves with the interests of the property-holders and voting for their political agents and executive committees (the modern capitalist State), the workers have been mixed up, with disastrous consequences, in the mercenary quarrels of their masters over property and trade routes in which the workers have no share whatever. Proof: The 10 years of war which left the workers, both in the " victorious " and the " defeated " countries alike poor, if not poorer than ever before. The present conflicts in Asia, Africa and elsewhere are of course no exception. The European, as well as the American and the Asiatic and African workers are all deluded in the belief that it is a struggle for their freedom. In reality, it is of course part and parcel of the eternal quarrels between rival groups of property-owners—hence of no concern to the propertyless working class. As an unknown poet sang during the first world-war :

" *Sing a song of Europe, highly civilized,*
" *Four and twenty nations, thoroughly hypnotized.*
" *When the battles opened, the bullets began to sing,*
" *Wasn't that a silly thing to do for any king?*
" *The kings were in the background, issuing commands,*
" *the queens were in their parlours, by etiquette's demands.*
" *The bankers in the counting-house busy multiplying,*
" *while all the rest were at the front, DOING ALL THE DYING.*"

That the teaching of Marx, which the S.P.G.B. and companion-parties elsewhere have been faithfully interpret-

ing and spreading for the past 50 years, should not yet have found a more universal echo and response among the working-class, we all regret of course. The reasons are manifold, not the least of which is our lack of means, and the prodigious means (including the poisonous Radiospider) at the disposal of the enemy. It cannot, however, discourage us from persevering on the straight and clean path we are pursuing, even if for the time being, we have to be content with the role of being just pioneers.

Upon returning to the Continent after world-war I, efforts, however feeble, were not wanting to make the founding of a revolutionary Socialist Party in England known over here. Comrades of the writer started a group in Dortmund, Germany, which however seems to have eventually disintegrated after the death of the more active members. Before anything could be got underway here in Austria, even the western pattern of democratic liberties was finally lost by the advent first of the Dollfuss-Schuschnigg dictatorship, then by Hitler and now by another occupation, so that for the last 20 years it has been virtually impossible to openly advocate the revolutionary socialist policy. I need hardly remind you of the fate awaiting anyone who exposes publicly in the Russian zone the fraud and maskerade labelled communism.

Personally I enjoy the satisfaction that I could contribute in England my own tiny share and have recorded in the SOCIALIST STANDARD my adherence to that great cause even before capitalism's great crisis and world-wars with atomic weapons had so glaringly demonstrated what capitalist greed, lust for power and domination is capable of and where what one of their most prominent representatives called " this appalling development " will land the human race, unless the workers of the world bestir themselves and join with us to end the nightmare. The Socialist Party of Great Britain points the scientific way how to dethrone the ruthless powers that impose upon the dispossessed the precarious and degrading conditions of existence—the wages-system—and how true Socialism will abolish it and ensure a dignified and enjoyable life for all.

R. F.

SOCIALIST STANDARD SUBSCRIPTION FORM

Detach and forward, with remittance, to Literature Secretary, S.P.G.B., 52, Clapham High Street, London, S.W.4.

Please send SOCIALIST STANDARD for 12 months (6 months, 2/9) for which 5/6 is enclosed.

Name ....
(BLOCK LETTERS)

Address ....

....

(State, if renewal, or new subscriber)

A. JACOBS

Very early in his working life Jacobs became interested in the struggles of the working class. As a young man he lived in Edmonton, then a rising suburb of North London.

By occupation a cigar maker, he had to make the journey daily to Battersea, in South London, having to rise early every morning to reach the workshop.

With ever-increasing numbers of workers on the platform, and few trains to take them, the workers were aroused into agitating for increased trains and workmen's facilities for cheap fares. Meetings were held, and into these Comrade Jacobs flung himself with zeal. One morning he was arrested on Liverpool Street Station and charged with disturbing the peace. His trial took place at the Guildhall, and he was defended by Mr. Thompson, at that time Editor of *Reynolds News,* and acquitted,

He was an active member of the Cigar Makers Union and served on their executive committee. Then he became interested in the propaganda of the old Social Democratic Federation and eventually joined them. At about this period of his life he experienced considerable unemployment and, with a young family, suffered chronic privation and want.

Very shortly after the formation of the S.P.G.B. he decided to join the Party following his resignation from the S.D.F.

For many years he was an enthusiastic worker and spoke at four, five and six meetings a week, very frequently addressing two meetings on Sundays. Following the outbreak of the war in 1914 he never hesitated to hold meetings in Victoria Park, East London, notwithstanding hostile demonstrations at every meeting he addressed.

When " peace " was declared he threw himself with redoubled energy once more into the struggle for Socialism, and only gave up owing to advancing age and decline in his health.

He became almost an institution on the meeting place in Victoria Park, for he seldom missed a meeting on Sundays during many years.

The Party has produced many great workers in its cause, but few gave more ungrudgingly than our old comrade.

He died in his 70th year, early in 1940.

C. F. C.

F. C. WATTS

F. C. Watts was an active member of the group that came out of the Social Democratic Federation to take part in the founding of our Party.

He was an excellent writer and contributed many articles on theoretical subjects to the SOCIALIST STANDARD as well as putting our position in written debates with opponents. He was also a good speaker; he spoke quietly and forcefully without indulging in rhetoric, and his lectures were packed with useful information and logical argument. He was particularly good when speaking on theoretical subjects.

For many years Watts conducted well attended classes on Economics at our various Head Offices; many writers and speakers, in the years before 1914, were greatly indebted to him for advice and for the information he so willingly imparted.

In the early years of the Party Watts undertook the work of keeping in touch with those abroad who were in sympathy with our outlook, and he contributed articles to the journal of the old Socialist Party of Canada *The Western Socialist.* He also translated a number of articles from foreign journals that had been written by prominent radical writers, such as Guesde.

Watts was a carver by trade, and a first class craftsman; some of the internal decorations of the ill-fated Titanic were his work, and he also did some of the carving on the coronation chair of George V.

Like Fitzgerald he was fond of cycling and till late in life he could be met on some of the interesting byways of England and in some of the quaint old inns.

Watts was active from the early days of the Party until late in the twenties; then he seems to have quietly faded out and we have not heard of him for many years.

It may interest those who have read our pamphlet " Socialism and Religion," to know that it was drafted by Watts. It was one of the most popular pamphlets, both here and in America, that the Party produced and a certain Bishop Brown quoted from it, and paid it a tribute, in his pamphlet " Christianism and Communism."

GILMAC.

We have reproduced an article contributed to the " Socialist Standard " in 1909. It will be seen that the main conclusions of this article are as fresh and pertinent to-day as when it was written. Time, that has played havoc with the parties that flourished at that period, has left the outlook we put forward still clear and sound.

THE COLLAPSE OF

DIRECT ACTION

"Industrial Unionism" is merely a pleasant name for Anarchism and "Direct Action." It is one of those almost inevitable elements of confusion and disorganisation which beset the working class in its advance. Every dog has its day, and every freak idea its boom, as though the workers were prepared to traverse every avenue of error before keeping steadily to the right road. The freak idea that the workers can, without the conquest of political power and by means of an industrial organisation alone, "take and hold" the means of life from the capitalists, is one that has just enjoyed its brief boom; but its hollowness has been quickly seen, and its followers have in consequence been rapidly dropping away.

The Industrial Unionists of this country being entirely unable to think out for themselves the adaptation of means to end that would be suitable to the situation here, have hitherto blindly followed in the unsteady footsteps of that peculiarly American organisation, the Industrial Workers of the World, and have added to the gaiety of life by their ludicrous attempt at copying that oranisation, from its structure even down to its slang. As things are going however, the British Industrialists seem likely to be hard put to it for something to imitate; and what will their " Union " do then, poor thing?

The Industrial Workers of the World, of Chicago and elsewhere goes from bad to worse. It still continues to propagate—by fission for while the total number of members in all the I.W.W.s grows less and less, the number of distinct and warring I.W.W.s multiplies apace. This suggests the not impossible outcome that in the near future the few remaining adherents of that idea will be each a separate I.W.W. unto himself.

The General Confederation of Labour of France has also until now been a source of joy and inspiration to the Industrialists because of the theatrical policy of the Anarchist section which has hitherto controlled it. The English Industrialists, indeed, are fond of speaking of the Confédération Générale du Travail as though it were a homogeneous body, when, in reality, it is, as its name implies, a heterogeneous agglomeration of unions and federations, each with its own rules, scales of subscription, and the like and comprising almost all shades of political opinion. But with that fine contempt for democracy which characterises the Anarchists, they have, until recently, bossed the French labour organisation, notwithstanding that they are a minority of the membership. The " blessed word " of the Anarchists is " liberty," but not the liberty of the greatest number, for that would be democracy, and therefore accursed. Thus in the General Confederation of Labour the voting for the administrators is by group, and not per member, and since the Anarchists are divided into many small groups, and the Socialists united into fewer large ones, the Anarchist minority has been able to govern the majority.

But now there are tears and curses in the Anarchist camp. Their candidates have been beaten, and by a majority which, though it appears small, represents in reality two-thirds of the membership. Niel, an opponent of the Anarchistic " Direct Action," has been elected secretary of the Confederation. The Guesdist organ, *Le Socialisme*, is naturally jubilant about it, and says " The Anarchist-Syndicalists," beaten twice by the election of Niel and of Thil, are again furious. The Confederal organisation was theirs. They thought it would endure so for ever, but they did not notice that their brutal authoritarianism had ended by disgusting even their friends. They believed that their electoral system would ensure their preponderance for ever, but they have been compelled to admit that even such a fantastic system may turn against them. And their chagrin equals their fury. The coarse abuse which their organ, the *Revolution*, pours out upon the " blacklegs " and " traitors " who have elected Niel will complete their discredit in trade union circles."

It will be seen that with the decline of the " Direct Action" movement in France and America the British Industrialists are in a sad plight. They are likely to be left entirely to their own mental resources, and the worst is to be feared for them. It is, indeed, inevitable that the neo-Anarchist movement should, in every country in which it appears, soon begin to fall to pieces of its own unsoundness and futility; while it is equally inevitable that the sound Socialist movement should, in every country on the globe, advance steadily and surely, even if slowly, step by step nearer to its triumph

F. C. WATTS.
(Socialist Standard April 1909).

(Non-members cordially invited to meetings. Inquiries should be addressed to Secretary at the addresses given below.)

BRISTOL.—Secretary : J. Flowers, 6, Backfields (off Upper York Street), Bristol. 2. Meets every 3rd Tuesday.

DUNDEE GROUP.—Meets Tuesdays at 7.30 p.m. at Woodworker's Hall, Coupars Alley, Wellgate. Correspondence to P. G. Cavanagh, 1b, Benvie Road, Dundee.

HERTS.—Secretary. B. M. Lloyd, 91, Attimore Road, Welwyn Garden City, Meeting, Room 2, Community Centre, Welwyn Garden City

HOUNSLOW.—Group meets every Monday at 8 p.m., at 16, Shirley Drive, Hounslow, Middlesex. Correspondence to J. Thurston at above address. Telephone : 7625 Hou.

OLDHAM.—Group meets Wednesdays 15th and 29th September, 7.30, at address of R. Lees, 35, Manchester St. Phone MAI 5165.

ROMFORD.—Group meets 2nd and 4th Friday each month at Church House, Wykeham Hall, Romford (8.0 p.m.) Correspondence to : C. C. Green, 12, Grosvenor Gardens, Upminster.

RUGBY.—Group meets alternate Mondays 6th and 20th August (or 4th and 18th October) at 7, Paradise Street. Correspondence : Sec. c o above address.

WATFORD.—Group meets alternate Thursdays 9th and 23rd September at 8 p.m., at T.U. Hall, Woodford Road, (near Junction Stn.) Enquiries to Sec. J. Lee, Ivy Cottage, Langley Hill, Kings Langley, Herts.

LECTURE AND DISCUSSION FULHAM BRANCH
at 691, Fulham Road, S.W.6,

Thursday, 16th September, at 8 p.m. (sharp).

" The Rationalist Press Association and the S.P.G.B."
—H. J. WILSON

DARTFORD BRANCH DISCUSSION
at
THE LABOUR CLUB,
Lowfield Street, Dartford.

Friday, October 9th—E. WILMOTT

"THE IMPLICATIONS OF THE MATERIALIST CONCEPTION OF HISTORY."

Questions and Discussion—Visitors Welcome

ISLINGTON PUBLIC MEETING
" THE SOCIALIST FUTURE "   Speaker : S. CASH

Wed. 15th Sept. 8 p.m.

ISLINGTON CENTRAL LIBRARY, HOLLOWAY ROAD.

ADMISSION FREE   **ADMISSION FREE**

LUNCH HOUR MEETINGS

Mondays :	Finsbury Square.
Tuesdays :	Lincoln's Inn Fields.
Wednesdays :	Finsbury Square.
Thursdays :	Tower Hill.
Fridays :	Lincoln's Inn Fields.

SPEAKERS FOR TRADE UNION BRANCHES.
Trade Union branches wishing to hear the Socialist Case are invited to apply to the Propaganda Committee at the Head Office or to a local branch.

BOREHAM WOOD
Will members and sympathisers willing to cooperate in forming a group at Boreham Wood contact :

I. WEBB, 52, Goldbeater Grove,
Burnt Oak, Edgware, Middlesex.

All meetings are open to the public and visitors are welcomed.

BIRMINGHAM meets Thursdays, 8.0 p.m., at " Bulls Head," Digbeth. Discussions 2nd and 4th Thursdays in month. Correspondence to Secretary, 69, Haslucks Green Road, Shirley, Birmingham.

BLOOMSBURY. Correspondence to Secretary, c o Conway Hall, Red Lion Square, W.C.1. September 9th and 23rd at 7.30 p.m.

BRADFORD AND DISTRICT. The branch Secretary will be very pleased to answer all enquiries. Write, Vera Barrett, 26, Harbour Crescent, Wibsey, Bradford or ring Bradford 71904 at any time.

BRIGHTON. Correspondence to Sec. D. Bown, 7a, Clifton Road, Brighton. Branch meets 4th Thursday each month at 7.30 p.m., Co-op Club 23, Hanover Crescent, The Level.

CAMBERWELL meets Thursdays at 8 p.m., " The Artichoke," Camberwell Church Street. Correspondence to Sec. I. Groves, 92, St. Georges Way, Peckham, S.E.15.

CROYDON meets every Wednesday, 8 p.m., at Ruskin House, Wellesley Rd., (nr. W. Croydon Station). Business and discussion meetings. All enquiries to Secretary, A. C. Wrenn, 28, Jasmine Grove, Penge, S.E.20.

DARTFORD meets every Friday at 8 p.m., Dartford Labour Club, Lowfield St., Dartford. Discussions after branch business. Sec. : H. J. Wilson, 7, Cyril Road, Bexleyheath, Kent. Tel. : Bexleyheath 1950.

EALING meets every Friday at 8 p.m. sharp, at The Memorial Hall, Windsor Road, Ealing (nr. Ealing Broadway). Correspondence to E. T. Critchfield, 48, Balfour Road, W.13.

ECCLES meets 2nd Friday in month, at 7.30 p.m., at 5, Gaskell Road, Eccles. Secretary, F. Lea.

FULHAM meets Thursdays, 8 p.m., 691, Fulham Road, S.W.6., (Nr. Parsons Green Stn.). Business and Discussion meetings. Correspondence to J. Keys, 6, Keppel House, Lucan Place, Chelsea, S.W.3.

GLASGOW (City) meets Wednesdays at 7.30 p.m., Workers Open Forum, Halls, Renfrew Street, C.2. Communications to Sec. R. Reid, 35, Eldon Street, Glasgow, C.3.

GLASGOW (Kelvingrove) meets alternate Mondays, 6th and 20th September, at 8 p.m., in St. Andrew's Hall, Berkeley Street (Door G). Communcations to J. Farmer, 46, Fernie Street, Glasgow, N.W.

HACKNEY meets Mondays at 8 p.m., at the Co-op Hall, 197, Mare Street, E.8. Letters to A. Ivemey, 99, Somerford Estate, Stoke Newington, N.16.

HAMPSTEAD meets Wednesdays, 8 p.m., at Blue Danube Club Restaurant, 153, Finchley Road, Hampstead. (Between Swiss Cottage and Finchley Road Met. Stn.). Enquiries to F. Webb, 52, Goldbeaters Grove, Edgware, Middlesex.

HIGH WYCOMBE Branch meets 1st and 3rd Thursdays, 7-9 p.m., discussion after Branch business. " The Nags Head," London Road, High Wycombe. Letters to Sec. J. E. Roe, 191, Bowerdean Road.

ISLINGTON meets Thursdays, 8 p.m., at Co-op Hall, 129, Seven Sisters Road, N.7. Lecture or discussion after Branch business. J. C. Rowan, 28, Redbourne Avenue, Finchley, N.3.

KINGSTON-ON-THAMES Sec., 19, Spencer Road, East Molesey (Tel. MOL 6492). Branch meets Thursday at 8 p.m. at above address.

LEWISHAM meets Mondays, 8 p.m., Co-op Hall, (Room 1) Davenport Road, Rushey Green, Catford, S.E.6. Sec. A. Fisher, 59a, Duncombe Hill, S.E.23.

LEYTON Branch meets Mondays 8.0 p.m., at Trades Hall, Grove House, High Road, Leyton, E.10. Lectures and Discussions held 2nd and 4th Monday in each month. Secretary, R. Coster, c o H.O., 52, Clapham High Street, S.W.4.

MANCHESTER Branch meets fortnightly Tuesdays, 7th and 21st September, George & Dragon Hotel, Bridge St.: Sec. J. M. Breakey, 2, Dennison Ave., Withington, Manchester, 20. Didsbury 5709.

NOTTINGHAM meets 1st and 3rd Wednesday in each month at the Peoples Hall, Heathcoat St., Nottingham, at 7.45 p.m. Sec. J. Clark, 82a Wellington Road, Burton-on-Trent.

PADDINGTON meets Wednesdays, 8.0 p.m., " Portman Arms," 422, Edgware Road, W.2. (4 mins. from " Met." Music Hall). Sec. T. J. Law, 180, Kilburn Park Road, N.W.6.

PALMERS GREEN Branch meets Thursdays, 7.30 p.m., Stirling House, Stuart Crescent, Wood Green, N.22. Letters to Sec., 18, Victoria Road, Edmonton, N.18.

ST. PANCRAS meets Fridays, 8 p.m., at Fred Tallant Hall, Drummond Street, Euston, N.W.1. Visitors welcomed. Discussions after branch business. Correspondence to Sec. c o Fred Tallant Hall.

S.W. LONDON meets Thursdays, 8 p.m., 52, Clapham High Street, S.W.4. Secretary, Joan Lestor, 59, Childebert Road, Balham, S.W.17.

SOUTHEND meets every Tuesday at 8 p.m., at Co-op Hall, Southchurch Road, Southend (entrance Essex St.). Visitors welcome. Enquiries to J. G. Grisley, 47, Eastbourne Grove, Westcliff-on-Sea, Essex.

SWANSEA Meets 2nd and 4th Sundays in month, 7-9.30 p.m., at Khayyam, Mansel Drive, Murton, Bishopston. Discussion after Branch business. Visitors welcomed. D. Jacobs, Secretary.

TOTTENHAM meets 2nd and 4th Thursdays in month, 8-10 p.m., West Green Library, Vincent Road, West Green Road, N.15. Communications to Secretary, E. Field, 18, Woodlands Park Road, N.15.

WEST HAM meets every Thursday at 8 p.m. at Salisbury Road Schools, Manor Park, E.12. Discussions after each meeting from 9 p.m. Communications to D. Deutz, 21, Kenilworth Gardens, Seven Kings, Essex.

WICKFORD meets every Thursday at 7.30 p.m., St. Edmunds Runwell Road, Wickford, Essex. Enquiries to Secretary, L. R. Plummer.

WOOLWICH meets 2nd and 4th Friday of month, 7 p.m. Town Social Club, Mason's Hill, S.E.18. Discussion after branch business. Outdoor meetings Sunday 6.30 p.m. Beresford Sq. Sec. H. C. Ramsay, 9, Milne Gardens, Eltham, S.E.9.

Published by The Socialist Party of Great Britain, 52, Clapham High Street, S.W.4 Printed for them by R. E. Taylor & Son. Ltd., 55-57, Banner Street, London, E.C.4 (T.U.)